HANDS-ON
STEAM
PLORATIONS
YOUNG LEARNERS

GRADES PRE-K–2

HANDS-ON STEAM EXPLORATIONS

FOR YOUNG LEARNERS

PROBLEM-BASED INVESTIGATIONS FOR PRESCHOOL TO SECOND GRADE

ALLISON BEMISS

PRUFROCK PRESS INC.
WACO, TEXAS

Edited by Stephanie McCauley

Cover design by Marjorie Parker and layout design by Allegra Denbo
Illustrations by Micah Benson

ISBN-13: 978-1-61821-746-2

Printed in the United States of America.

At the time of this book's publication, all facts and figures cited are the most current available. All telephone numbers, addresses, and website URLs are accurate and active. All publications, organizations, websites, and other resources exist as described in the book, and all have been verified. The author and Prufrock Press Inc. make no warranty or guarantee concerning the information and materials given out by organizations or content found at websites, and we are not responsible for any changes that occur after this book's publication. If you find an error, please contact Prufrock Press Inc.

Prufrock Press Inc.
P.O. Box 8813
Waco, TX 76714-8813
Phone: (800) 998-2208
Fax: (800) 240-0333
http://www.prufrock.com

TABLE OF CONTENTS

INTRODUCTION

Encouraging Big Ideas From Little Learners

OVERVIEW

Young children are natural scientists. Little learners play, explore, and test with wonder as a guide to learning. In order to encourage innovative thinking, we must offer our youngest learners opportunities to nurture these skills while solving problems. This book, *Hands-On STEAM Explorations for Young Learners*, shares 10 STEAM (science, technology, engineering, arts, and mathematics) investigations based on popular nursery rhymes that little learners (and adults) know and love. Several critical factors, such as learning environment, growth mindset, innovation strategies, personalized learning, and early childhood standards, should be considered to effectively reach the unique needs of each young learner.

ENVIRONMENTS FOR EXPLORING

Physical Environment

The physical environment of an early childhood classroom should be one that allows the child to be as independent as possible. We want to be sure that materials, tools, tables, and chairs are at the appropriate level. First and foremost, ensure that all materials, including those used in STEAM investigations, are appropriate for students ages 3 and up. The nursery rhyme-themed challenges in the 10 lessons in this book all provide the opportunity for students to make age-appropriate choices as they plan, design, and create.

One way to help students is by organizing materials so that they can easily see in a very concrete way what they are selecting. For example, rather than circling on a piece of paper the materials they will use, let them first actually see (and touch, if necessary) the materials they have access to. (See the Teacher's Lesson Guide for more information on how to organize materials within each lesson.) Labeling with pictures and words is also an important component for the early childhood classroom. This not only promotes literacy,

1

but also helps the little learner be more independent as he or she selects materials and cleans up—which brings us to the last, but most important, point of this section. We want students to be responsible for as much of the cleanup as safely possible; therefore, they will need access to brooms, dustpans, water, sponges, and other cleaning materials. The students need to "own" their classroom. Learning to take care of their environment is a part of building responsibility and creating a sense of community.

> The students need to "own" their classroom. Learning to take care of their environment is a part of building responsibility and creating a sense of community.

STEAM Investigation Guidelines

STEAM investigation guidelines and lab safety are critical components of the classroom environment. When working with young learners, make safety as clear and easy to understand as possible. Posting the following guidelines in the classroom and reviewing them prior to each lesson will help students remember how to play and explore safely:

L: Learn by exploring!
(Trying and failing is learning; failing to try is not.)

A: Always keep materials *away* from your eyes, nose, mouth, and hands.
(As needed, wear safety goggles and gloves to keep your body safe.)

B: Be aware.
(Notice what's happening around you.)

Emotional Environment

The emotional environment of a classroom is very important to learning, and this is especially true in STEAM challenges like those in this book. Students will be required to share, collaborate, and communicate in every investigation in this book. This is an important lifelong skill for our young learners to begin practicing. In order to make this happen, students need to be working in an environment that supports their needs. If we think of Maslow's Hierarchy of Needs (1943), we know that students need to first feel safe and secure before they can advance to the higher levels of thinking. Our little learners need a sense of belonging in the classroom. *Life in a Crowded Place* by Ralph Peterson (1992) shared many ways that we, as educators, can make a learning community. Peterson suggested that teachers should facilitate their classroom to be more like a family. Two ideas in particular he discussed involve creating routines and celebrations to help build a community of learners. Each of the nursery rhyme challenge investigations offers an opportunity for learners to follow a specific routine and communication pattern, like the curiosity catchphrases and partner talks. There are also celebrations of learning that occur during each lesson as the students share their creations or thinking. For example, each time a lesson calls for a Scientist Stroll (see the Teacher's Lesson Guide), this is a celebration of new learning. It is important to communicate these celebrations of learning with students.

Be an engineer (or scientist, artist, mathematician, etc.). Several lessons instruct the teacher to encourage children to do things like "put on engineer eyes" or "listen with engineer ears." These phrases help the students understand that engineers (and scientists, mathematicians, and artists) use their senses to make observations, solve problems, and create. We also want to encourage students to see themselves in these roles; therefore, telling them to become a STEAM professional in this simple way helps to create a community of scientific thinkers, makers, and problem solvers.

Mistake Makers and Innovative Thinkers

Mistakes mean you are learning, but it doesn't always feel this way. Even to young students, mistakes feel negative. You can help change this thinking in two simple ways:

1. **Celebrating mistakes as learning and sharing your own mistakes.** Young students learn so much from what we model, both intentionally and unintentionally.
2. **Giving feedback to students by placing the value on thinking rather than knowing.** You can do this by having students share examples of mistakes they made and what they learned, rather than only sharing what they learned. This simple change can completely change the class mindset on mistakes. *Mindsets in the Classroom* by

Mary Cay Ricci (2017) shares many more ideas on creating a classroom with a growth mindset.

The five curiosity catchphrases used in this book are specific strategies designed to model and encourage innovative thinking for young students. The catchphrases were influenced by the ideas and beliefs found in *Mindsets in the Classroom* (Ricci, 2017), *Strategies That Work* (Harvey & Goudvis, 2007), and *Creating Innovators* (Wagner, 2012). The following models of higher order thinking and innovation in education also impacted this book: Bloom's taxonomy (1956), the Innovation Model (Project GEMS, 2011), Design Thinking (Stanford d.school, n.d.), and Sheffield's (2003) heuristic for creative and innovative mathematicians.

Personalizing Learning

Our education world is filled with many acronyms—GT, PTP, IEP, 2e, ELL, RtI—that sum up to one basic idea: personalized learning. Dr. Julia Roberts and Dr. Tracy Inman (2015) discussed the notion of there being no such thing as a "one-size-fits-all" lesson or classroom for students in their book *Strategies for Differentiating Instruction*. Roberts and Inman went on to note that the ultimate goal of differentiation is to create lifelong learners. The minds-on, hands-on investigations in this book offer natural opportunities for lifelong learning by differentiating through task. Although at first glance it may appear that everyone is doing the same work, that is not the case. When we think of differentiation or personalization, that means the teacher is intentionally matching the readiness level of the child to the content he or she is exploring. The explorations in this book are personalized for each learner because the challenges are set up as opened-ended tasks, with multiple approaches and many possible answers. This format offers a natural opportunity for students to take their language, content, and thinking to their own levels of readiness, wherever they may be.

The explorations in this book are personalized for each learner because the challenges are set up as opened-ended tasks, with multiple approaches and many possible answers.

STANDARDS ADDRESSED
IN THIS BOOK

Common Core State Standards for Mathematical Practice

1. Make sense of problems and persevere in solving them.
2. Reason abstractly and quantitatively.
3. Construct viable arguments and critique the reasoning of others.
4. Model with mathematics.
5. Use appropriate tools strategically.
6. Attend to precision.
7. Look for and make use of structure.
8. Look for and express regularity in repeated reasoning.

Next Generation Science Standards: K–2 Engineering Design

Students who demonstrate understanding can do the following:
-   K-2 ETS 1-1 Ask questions, make observations, and gather information about a situation people want to change to define a simple problem that can be solved through a new or improved object or tool.
-   K-2 ETS 1-2 Develop a simple sketch, drawing, or physical model to illustrate how the shape of an object helps it function as needed to help solve a given problem.

Common Core State Standards for English Language Arts: Speaking and Listening

Comprehension and Collaboration:
-   CCSS.ELA-LITERACY.SL. (K.1, 1.1, and 2.1) Participate in collaborative conversations with diverse partners about (grade level) topics and texts with peers and adults in small and larger groups.

TEACHER'S LESSON GUIDE

Nursery rhymes have been used for years to help young students learn to read and practice fluency. This book expands on that idea by using a nursery rhyme for each investigation as the hook for a language and literacy mini-lesson, and as the background information for each of the STEAM challenges the students will work to solve.

STEAM CHALLENGES

Each STEAM challenge in this curriculum sets the stage for a problem the students will work to solve for the characters of the nursery rhyme. It is the hook that draws the student into the science, arts, and mathematics content. Each STEAM challenge is formatted using similar components explained in the following sections. Using a similar format for each investigation helps children (and teachers) develop a routine, anticipate procedures, and problem solve.

Goals and Objectives

Three student goals are listed in each exploration. Some of the goals are related to specific STEAM content, while others are focused on thinking processes like making observations, connections, and asking questions. The goals in these investigations are related to broader standards and practices, including the Common Core State Standards for Mathematical Practice, the Next Generation Science Standards for K–2 Engineering Design, and the Common Core State Standards for English Language Arts for K–2 Speaking and Listening.

Materials

The majority of the materials included in each of these lessons are items that can be found at the grocery store or dollar market. If the lesson requests

materials that you cannot find, do not let that steer you away from the lesson. Many lessons offer options for substitution. On that same note, please do not let the number of materials steer you away from the lesson. Adapt the materials list as needed. The number of materials used in a project or the final "look" of the project is not what is most important; it is the thinking and problem solving opportunities we want students to experience.

Organization. Materials should be sorted and organized for the students in trays, bowls, bags, or other containers. This will help them as they plan and make choices. Container ideas include the following:

- plastic chip and dip trays,
- bento-style boxes,
- small buckets or tubs on trays,
- clear plastic punch cups, and
- plastic shower caddies.

Important Investigation Ideas to Note

The ideas listed in this section offer background information on the investigation for the teacher. This section shares examples of how the lesson connects to the real world and/or content that the students will explore later in their educational careers. Students are not expected to master all of the content summarized in this section. This area is to provide you, the teacher, with a quick "brushup" of science content explored in the lesson. Another purpose of this section is to help you advocate for minds-on, hands-on learning opportunities. Sometimes when people see students playing and exploring to solve a problem, they see it only as play, without fully understanding the deeper levels of thinking. This section will help you share with others exactly what your students are learning and how it relates to the "big picture" of content they will learn throughout their education. Early childhood teachers have the important job of laying the foundation for all other learning.

Language and Literacy

Curiosity catchphrases. Curiosity catchphrases are one of the most important components of the exploration process. They provide a way for the students to think at high levels, as well as serve as a scaffold for language. By providing the following sentence starters, we help students access thinking and learn to share it with others:

- *I wonder . . .* (Questioning)
- *I notice . . .* (Making observations)
- *I think if . . .* (Predicting, inference)
- *This reminds me of . . .* (Connecting to schema)
- *Oops, I learned . . .* (Growth mindset)

Vocabulary. The vocabulary in this lesson is both for the teacher and the student. It is helpful if the teacher models these words both in the introduction and the investigation portion of the lesson plan. The students will then start to use the words as they investigate, reflect, and wonder. Although vocabulary is included in the rubric, this is *not* for a formal assessment. Teachers will just want to note which words students are beginning to own and which to continue modeling.

Speaking and listening. In this part of the lesson, students will always begin with choral reading (reading as a whole class) or singing the rhyme together. Then the students will discuss the rhyme to either deepen comprehension or understand poetic devices. This section also provides students with the opportunity to practice speaking and sharing ideas and listening to and respecting the ideas of others.

Partner Talk is first used in this section. Partner Talk is a strategy listed by the National Council of Teachers of English as a strategy to strengthen collaboration and understanding (Simon, n.d.). In this curriculum, classes will adapt some of the steps of Partner Talk to think and share:

1. Pose the question.
2. Allow wait time for students to think independently.
3. Students take turns sharing ideas with one another.
4. Students share ideas with the class. (Students can either share their own ideas or their partners' ideas.)

EDUCATOR'S TOOLBOX

Introduction

In the introduction of each lesson, the teacher will share the STEAM challenge the students will work to solve in the investigation. Some lessons also

include mini-lessons to help build prior knowledge and experiences that the students will need in order to solve the investigation.

Investigation Procedure

Play, explore, and create! The students will be engaged in solving the problem in this portion of the lesson. Each lesson sets this up a little differently. In some challenges, investigating will be done independently or in pairs, while others are done in small groups with the teacher. This grouping pattern can always be changed to match the needs and readiness level of the students you serve.

Many people think that wondering should only occur at the beginning of a lesson; however, the truth is that the more you know, the more you wonder!

Reflection

Reflection is an important part of learning that is sometimes overlooked. Each lesson includes an intentional reflection time for the students to think about what they have learned.

Scientist Stroll. This strategy is based off of the strategy called *gallery walk*, where a teacher will post several questions around the room and small groups move around the room to answer questions together (Francek, 2006). In this curriculum, students use the Scientist Stroll to move around the room to observe, wonder, and share. Rather than looking at posed questions on chart paper, the students will display their projects as they walk around the room to view others' projects. Teachers can choose to make this a view-only or a hands-on experience, depending on the needs of the class.

Wondering

Many people think that wondering should only occur at the beginning of a lesson; however, the truth is that the more you know, the more you wonder!

Therefore, it is a good idea to give students an opportunity to wonder and share those questions at the end of a lesson. This encourages students to push deeper into the content and design process through curiosity, an important lifelong skill we want to help our young students learn.

STUDENT'S TOOLBOX

The student's toolbox is a summarized version of the lesson plan that can be distributed as a handout. The student's toolbox will work best for children who are readers. The toolbox is an additional resource for the classroom. With younger students, this handout could be used to help communicate with families. Many of these minds-on, hands-on investigations work well for family STEAM events.

RUBRIC: WHAT'S HAPPENING IN THIS STEAM INVESTIGATION?

The rubric is included to help educators know what to look for in each lesson. It provides a summary of what you should see and hear when you walk into a classroom exploring these STEAM investigations. Jotting down students' quotes or observations on the rubric will help you recognize change and growth over time. There is not a specific set of instructions in the lesson plan for when to use the rubric. You may choose to highlight or write on the rubrics as you walk around and listen to the students explore in the investigation, or you may choose to use them as a reflection at the end of the investigation. Use whatever method you find works best for you in that lesson. The rubric might also be a helpful piece of evidence to share with fellow educators, students, and families as you reflect on the experiences and learning opportunities provided in each investigation.

EXPLORATION

Hickory, Dickory, Dock: *Friction*

Hickory, dickory, dock,
The mouse ran up the clock,
The clock struck one,
The mouse ran down,
Hickory, dickory, dock.

STEAM CHALLENGE

The chime is ringing. The clock struck one. The mice are panicked. Everyone knows the cat wakes to prowl the house at one o'clock. Yet, the mice can't seem to make it down the clock quick enough each night. They have started to use toy cars to zoom down the ramp, but they still can't seem to beat the cat. Your mission is to see if you can help the mice get down the clock ramp quickly and safely.

Goals and Objectives

During this exploration, students will:
- ask wondering questions to guide their exploration,
- investigate force and motion in order to build schema, and
- analyze data collected during the investigation to determine the best choice of ramp covering and slope for the Hickory, Dickory, Dock mice.

Materials

Note. The following materials are needed per small group or pair of students.
- Handout 1.1: Student's Toolbox
- Handout 1.2: Ramp Test Data Collection Sheet
- 2 identical pieces of wood or cardboard (suggested size: 5.5 in. x 36 in.) propped up on 3–5 books
- A picture of a clock face to attach to the top of the ramp (optional)
- 2 toy mice (or small pieces of rolled fabric with pipe cleaner whiskers and tails)
- 2 identical toy cars
- Rubber band or yarn to tie the mouse onto the car (optional)
- Ramp coverings: sandpaper, aluminum foil, cotton batting, carpet strip, etc.
- Plastic clamps or extra-large binder clips
- Yardstick or ruler
- Crayons

Important Investigation Ideas to Note

Students will explore physics and engineering in this investigation. As the students test which material helps the mice move down the ramp the fastest, they are exploring inclined planes, slope, friction, gravity, and Newton's first and second laws of motion. The goal is not for the students to have complete mastery of these concepts by the end of this investigation, but rather to build schema or a basic understanding of how objects move. This prior knowledge will serve them well later in life when they explore physics in upper grades. It provides an anchor experience for new learning to latch on to later.

- **Newton's First Law of Motion:** An object at rest will stay at rest, and an object in motion will stay in motion unless acted on by an unbalanced force. Newton's first law is sometimes called the Law of Inertia.
- **Newton's Second Law of Motion:** The acceleration of an object is equal to the net force applied to the object divided by the mass of the object. In other words, the more mass an object has, the more force it will take to accelerate it. It also means that the harder you push or pull an object, the faster it will go. In the introduction for this investigation, the students will see how adjusting the height of the ramp impacts the acceleration of the mouse car. The higher the ramp, the more closely it follows the direction of gravity; therefore, the faster the mouse will make it down the clock ramp.

Language and Literacy

Curiosity Catchphrase

- *I wonder . . .*

Vocabulary

- Friction
- Motion
- Inclined plane/ramp
- Push or pull (Force)
- Gravity

Speaking and Listening

- What is this nursery rhyme about?
    - Read the poem aloud once to the students and then choral read the rhyme together as a class.
    - Partner Talk: What is this nursery rhyme about? (Mice race down the clock.)
    - Let the students share their answers with the whole group.

- Why do you think the mice run down the clock?
    - Partner Talk: Why do you think the mice run down the clock? (There is no right or wrong answer for this question. The students will use their imaginations to explore possibilities. Examples might include: "The clock chime was loud and scared the mouse," or "The mouse needed to go to bed.")
    - Have students share their partners' ideas, rather than their own. This serves as a model for students of how to listen to others and value the thoughts and ideas of their classmates.

EDUCATOR'S TOOLBOX

Introduction

Tell the students that you have the answer to why the mice race down the clock at one o'clock, and it is a big part of today's STEAM challenge. Read the STEAM challenge card to the students (see Appendix).

Inertia Mini-Lesson

- Show students the ramp with the clock face and tell them this is the ramp, or inclined plane, that the mice are trying to race down every night. Lay the clock ramp board flat on the ground. Place the mouse in the car on the top of the clock face.
- Ask a student to tell you what is happening. He or she may say "nothing." Explain that although it looks like nothing is happening, there is actually more going on. What students see now is an example of inertia. Say "inertia" and ask them repeat it, letting them give the word a

try. Young minds and mouths often love to try new words—especially long academic-sounding words.

- Say: *Inertia sounds like a hard word, but you've already observed it. If I told you this mouse is showing us an example of inertia, what do you think inertia means?* Listen for their answers. If students are hesitant, have them tell you again what the mouse is doing (e.g., "The mouse is sitting on the board," or "The mouse is not moving"). Tell them *inertia* means that the mouse will keep doing exactly what it's doing unless something pushes or pulls it. A push or a pull is a force.
- Have a few students come to the front of the class and demonstrate a push and a pull while the clock ramp board is still flat on the ground. Before students apply any force to the mouse car, have them share the type of force they plan to use (e.g., "I will pull the car along the board"). Repeat this phrase for each student who tries out the force.
- Ask the class: *If inertia means that an object (in our case the mouse car) will keep doing what it is doing, then why do our cars stop after they travel across the floor? What makes them stop?* For example, if the car hit a chair, explain to the students that the chair pushed back on the car, making it stop.

Gravity Mini-Lesson

- Do another test where the car comes to a stop on its own. Explain that a special force called *gravity* is always pulling us down toward the center of the Earth. (A globe might be useful, if students have a hard time visualizing this idea.) If gravity is a new word for them, let them practice saying it.
- Set the car back on the ramp. Say: *When the mouse car is at rest and not moving, how do we know that gravity is still pulling down on the car?* Expand on this idea by giving the car a push and asking: *Even when I push the car forward, how do I know gravity is still pulling down on the car?*
- Tell students: *You might have noticed that in our challenge the mice aren't traveling on a flat board like we have explored in class today. They are on a ramp, or an inclined plane.*
- Prop the clock ramp up at an angle on several thick books or a table. Ask what the students predict will happen when you put the car on top of the ramp. Because most students have had experience playing with blocks or cars, they may correctly predict that the car will move down the ramp. However, do not tell them if they are right or wrong in their

prediction. Instead, tell them that today they will be engineers, or people who design, problem solve, and construct things like buildings and bridges. Say that engineers always test their predictions.

- Have the students share their predictions by using the "*I wonder . . .*" curiosity catchphrase, coming up to the ramp, and testing their ideas (e.g., "I wonder if we prop the ramp up on the table, will the car zoom down the ramp?"). Ask the other students to put on "engineer eyes" and watch what they see happening as the student tests his or her theory. Let the students share their observations.

- Move the ramp higher so that it has a greater slope. Ask the students what they think will happen if you raise the ramp. Repeat the same process as before, letting the students practice making predictions using the "*I wonder . . .*" curiosity catchphrase (e.g., "I wonder if we raise the ramp, will the mouse car move faster?"). The students will notice the car should move faster down the ramp.

- Lower the ramp and repeat the same process, letting students share their predictions, thinking, and observations. Repeat this until you believe that students are starting to notice the pattern that when you raise the ramp, the car moves faster down the ramp, and when you lower the ramp, it takes the car longer to reach the bottom. Help students verbalize this generalization.

- Ask students what they think will happen if you hold the ramp straight up. Repeat the same test procedure with the ramp perpendicular to the ground. The car will fall straight down. Ask the students what force is pulling the car (gravity).

- Ask them what force they predict is pulling the car when it goes down the ramp at an angle. Show them again if necessary. Tell them that gravity is always pulling the car down, but when the ramp is not there, or it is straight up and down, the car doesn't have anything to resist the force of gravity, so it falls straight down to the ground.

- Say: *So if your only concern were getting the mice down quickly, how would you angle the ramp?* Students might say, "We would want the ramp almost straight up and down." Say: *But when we reread our challenge, it doesn't only say to get the mice down quickly. It also states that we need to get the mice down safely.* Tell the students that there are special engineers called *safety engineers* who are responsible for making sure that people stay safe. Ask them to choose an angle that they think will keep the mice safe but also let them get down pretty quickly.

Friction Mini-Lesson

- Adjust the ramp on a table or a stack of books at an angle that the students choose. The ramp should not need to be held. Choose an angle that still has the mice going down pretty quickly in order for the following friction test to be engaging for the students.
- Pull out a box filled with the various friction test coverings (e.g., sandpaper, carpet strip, aluminum foil, etc.). Explain to the students that you are in on a little secret the mice don't want the cat to know. The mice found more than just a toy car to help them with their journey; they also found all of the materials in this box. Pull out each item one at a time to show your students.
- Show the students the clamps or binder clips. Ask them to predict why the mice might have included something like that in their box. You can also model this thinking by saying: *I'm wondering if the mice included plastic clamps with the sandpaper, foil, and cotton because they meant for us to use them to hold the materials on the board. Let's give it a test.* Demonstrate how the clamps or binder clips work to hold the material on the board.
- Put the students in groups of two or three. Ask them to partner talk to discuss this wondering: *I wonder why the mice thought these fabrics might help them move faster or more safely down the ramp.* After all students have had time to think individually and partner talk, let them share their ideas with the class. A sample response might be, "I think if we put the sandpaper on the ramp it will help the mouse car move down faster than the aluminum foil." (*Note.* Please remember it does not matter if their predictions are correct. We never want to correct a student's prediction; we want to encourage students to test their ideas and learn from mistakes and observations.)
- Get out a second clock ramp to test one of the student predictions. If a student believes aluminum foil will be a faster option for the mice than sandpaper, cover one ramp with aluminum foil and one with sandpaper, and then release the two cars at the same time. This allows the students to easily observe with their "engineer eyes" how the covering impacts the speed of the cars. It is important that the mouse cars be identical. Due to Newton's second law of motion, a change in mass will impact the acceleration of the cars. If you use two different car models, one might have a greater mass than the other.

- While observing this test, the students will notice that the covering will change the speed of the car. Pass around the materials to let the students name the properties (or attributes) of each material. They may notice that foil is smooth, while sandpaper is bumpy.

- Have the students rub their hands together very quickly and explain what they feel. They will probably say their hands get warmer. Tell them this is something called *friction*. Like you did with inertia, let them practice saying the word. Friction is a force that acts in the opposite direction of the movement; therefore, it slows the car down. Tell them that today they will want to watch for patterns to see if one of the materials helps the car slow down or if one helps the car move faster.

Investigation Procedure

1. Give each group two identical clock ramps and two identical mouse cars. Explain that because they will be comparing speed, students will need two ramps to do the investigation.

2. Give each group copies of Handout 1.1: Student's Toolbox to guide their investigation and Handout 1.2: Ramp Test Data Collection Sheet to collect their observations.

3. The students should begin by deciding how high they want to adjust the ramps. They may need to explore for a few minutes, repeating some of the steps of the gravity mini-lesson in order to determine the height. Handout 1.2 includes a place for students to record the height of the ramps. If students are ready for the challenge of using a yard-stick to measure how many inches the ramps are off the floor, they can write that down. Or they can include an informal measurement by writing or drawing something, such as a desk, seat of a chair, or five unit blocks from a block center. This can easily be personalized based on your students' needs.

4. Before students begin working, remind them that you want them to be watching with their "engineer eyes" to see that the mice are making it down safely. You also want them listening with "engineer ears" for physics words like *force, push, pull, gravity,* and *friction.*

5. Once each group has determined the height of their clock ramps, tell them the height must stay the same for the remainder of the exploration.

6. After groups have set the height, give each group a box or bag with ramp coverings and clamps.

7. As the teacher, your job is now to stand back, watch, and listen. When invited by a group, you can play and explore with them, but you should be modeling the learning process rather than telling students the answers. For example, you might say: *I wonder if crumpling the aluminum foil before we add it to the board might slow the car down because it will be bumpy, like driving through gravel.*

8. Listen to their problems. Ask questions that make them push further to solve a problem: *I understand it's frustrating that the cotton batting is making the car slide off the ramp. How might you adjust the design to keep the car on the road? Based on what you've seen in this test, if you were a safety engineer, would you recommend using cotton batting on the ramp?*

9. Handout 1.2 gives students a place to record three different tests; however, encourage them to try more than that if they have more time.

10. If a group finishes early, have them tell you not only about what they tested, but also what they learned along the way. Students can modify the curiosity catchphrase by saying "I wondered _____ , and I learned _____ ."

Reflect

- Have the students circle the test data on Handout 1.2 that they feel is the fastest and safest choice for the mouse car. Then ask them to set their ramps up to do that test again.

- Let the students do a Scientist Stroll to take a look at other groups' tests. It is a great idea to let the groups do a test on another group's ramp to see if they learn anything new. Remember that groups might have different coverings, or they may have their ramps at different heights, so there is an opportunity for new learning by exploring others' designs.

- Have the students tell what they noticed using their "engineer eyes" about tests they did on other groups' clock ramps. They might share ways their test results were alike, different, or surprising. Maybe they see that a lower ramp had a similar result to theirs, but the car rolled much slower. Maybe they are surprised that a group crumpled its foil to make a bumpy surface.

- Tell the students you heard them use some of the physics words you'd asked them to listen for with their "engineer ears" during their investigation. Ask for the students to tell you any examples they used or heard a friend use. Repeat the vocabulary—*push, pull, gravity,* and *friction*—if needed. If students are unable to share many examples, model some for them using their mouse ramps.
- Remind the students they were not only engineers today, but also safety engineers. Ask them why it is important to have safety engineers to check for the safety of products that we use, like cars or playground equipment.
- Ask them why adding the word *safety* made the challenge a little harder than just trying to get down as fast as possible. (The fastest option would be to just let the car drop straight down with the pull of gravity; however, this is not the safest choice for the mice.)
- Ask if they noticed any patterns today about coverings that repeatedly made the cars slow down. They will probably notice that materials like cotton batting or carpet will cause the car to slow down more than smooth materials.
- Partner Talk: How could friction help keep the mice safer on their journey? (It slows down the mice as they come down the ramp.)
- Encourage the students to share their answers with the class.

Wonder

- Ask the students to tell you what they wonder now that they've solved the mice's problem. For example, a student might say, "I know that smooth or flat foil was faster than crumpled foil. Now I wonder what would happen if I used sandpaper with foil on top of it."
- Adding the materials for this lesson to your science center will give students the opportunity to test out their wonderings on another day.

Additional Literature Connections and Resources

Ferrie, C. (2017). *Newtonian physics for babies*. Chicago, IL: Sourcebooks.

Newtonian Physics for Babies provides simple explanations and diagrams for complex concepts that help young children (and adults) better understand physics.

Pascal, J. B. (2014). *Who was Isaac Newton?* New York, NY: Grossett & Dunlap.

Who Was Isaac Newton? is a chapter book that shares information on Isaac Newton's life and scientific theories and discoveries.

STUDENT'S TOOLBOX

👁 **ENGINEER EYES:**
How is the mouse car moving? What is the speed of the mouse car? Is the mouse safe?

👂 **ENGINEER EARS:**
Listen for your friends to say our physics words like *force*, *motion*, *push*, *pull*, and *friction*, and our curiosity catchphrase, "*I wonder . . .*"

1. Choose a height for your clock ramps.

2. Record the height on Handout 1.2. (*Note.* Once the height is recorded, it cannot be changed.)

3. Take a peek at your ramp coverings. Feel them. What do you notice?

4. Use your catchphrase "*I wonder . . .*" as you explore and try new ideas.

5. Set up your clock ramps to match your catchphrase. For example, if you wonder if sandpaper will make the car move faster than cotton, then you should have cotton on one ramp and sandpaper on the other.

6. Investigate and test!

7. Record your results.

8. Repeat steps 4–7 again and again, until time is up! Remember to use your catchphrase and try to listen for your physics vocabulary.

9. If you've used all of the materials just as they are, you might think you are done, but you're not! Just think about how you can change them and try again. Can you cut, crumple, or tear a material to do a different test? Your imagination is the limit here. Don't give up.

10. **Partner/Group Talk:** Which covering made the safest and fastest journey for the mouse?

11. Circle that answer on your group's handout and set up the ramps to test that combination again. For example, if you believe that sandpaper made for the fastest and safest journey, that's what you'd set up on your board.

12. **Finish this sentence:** One thing that surprised me in this challenge was _____ !

13. **Partner Talk:** How could friction help keep the mice safer on their journey?

14. What do you wonder now?

RAMP TEST DATA COLLECTION SHEET

Directions: Draw and label each ramp covering. Color the ramp covering that was the "winner" for each test. When you have finished your tests, circle the ramp covering you tested that is the best choice for the mice.

Height of Ramps = _____

Test	Ramp 1	Ramp 2
1		

EXPLORATION 1: HICKORY, DICKORY, DOCK

Name: _____ Date: _____

Test	Ramp 1	Ramp 2
2		
3		

EXPLORATION 1: HICKORY, DICKORY, DOCK

STEAM

Name: _____ Date: _____

WHAT'S HAPPENING IN THIS STEAM INVESTIGATION?

	Teacher	Student
Looks Like	- Moving around the room observing group work - Listening to student language, making notes of vocabulary or curiosity catchphrases used (nonevaluative)	- Testing different coverings - Listening to and watching group members as they work together - Recording findings on Handout 1.2
Sounds Like	- Choral reading the nursery rhyme - Modeling vocabulary and the curiosity catchphrase while observing group work - Asking questions to require students to dig deeper, make connections, or try again	- Choral reading nursery rhyme - Sharing observations using the "*I wonder . . .*" curiosity catchphrase - Using vocabulary (*push, pull, gravity, friction, motion, inclined plane/ ramp*) while designing, predicting, testing, and recording findings - Sharing ideas, mistakes, and new learning

EXPLORATION

2

Did You Ever See a Lassie?: *Relative Location*

Did you ever see a lassie?
A lassie, a lassie?
Did you ever see a lassie
Go this way and that?
Go this way and that way,
Go this way and that way.
Did you ever see a lassie
Go this way and that?

STEAM CHALLENGE

Help! Lassie is in a new town, and the map app on her phone has gone haywire. Now she is lost! She's stuck going this way and that way. Your mission is to create a 3-D path to help Lassie find her way back home.

Goals and Objectives

During this exploration, students will:
- make observations to help identify and solve problems,
- create a path using spatial visualization skills and vocabulary to plan and map the city, and
- brainstorm and share ideas with peers and the teacher, working in small and large groups.

Materials

Note. The following materials are needed per small group of students.
- Handout 2.1: Student's Toolbox
- Large piece of cardboard or foam board
- Construction paper
- Cardboard tubes
- Aluminum foil
- Funnels
- Masking tape
- Ping-Pong or rubber bouncy ball (to serve as Lassie)
- Scissors
- Markers or crayons
- Masking tape

Important Investigation Ideas to Note

Students will explore engineering and design concepts in this investigation. Completing the steps will give the students an opportunity to continue exploring what they learned about force and motion in Exploration 1. They will extend on previous learning by having the opportunity to explore what happens when an object in motion stops. Students will need to problem solve, making adjustments to the slope and size of their tubes to get the balls moving again using gravity.

This investigation also gives students another glimpse of STEAM careers like civil engineering. Civil engineers have a very important job that young students are often interested in when they see large construction equipment or explore in the block center. Civil engineers are responsible for the design, construction, and maintenance of roads, bridges, dams, and buildings in cities. Engineers are required to use spatial reasoning to visualize three-dimensional cities and problem solve as they design and make plans for towns and cities. According to the admissions information website for the Cockrell School of Engineering at the University of Texas at Austin (n.d.), this visual processing skill is something that is sometimes overlooked in mathematics instruction. The good news is that you can change that! Spatial reasoning, or spatial visualization, as it is sometimes called, can be improved through play-based activities like this one. If you find your students are struggling with this skill, playing with blocks has been found to help improve their understanding of spatial concepts (Fischer, 2011).

Language and Literacy

Curiosity Catchphrase

- *I notice . . .*

Vocabulary

- Relative location (e.g., right, left, beside, behind, next to, inside, near, between)

Speaking and Listening

- Who is this nursery rhyme about?
  - Read the poem aloud, and then choral read or sing it together.
  - Partner Talk: Who is this nursery rhyme about? (Lassie.)
  - Tell the students that the word *lassie* is a special word that is a synonym for another word. (Explain that *synonym* means that two words have the same meaning.) Ask if anyone knows the synonym for the word *lassie*. If not, tell them that lassie is a word that is used in Scotland and Ireland to mean "girl."

- Introduce the word *laddie*. Ask students to partner talk with a friend near them to make a prediction of what laddie might mean. If needed, prompt them with the cue, "If lassie means girl, then laddie means _____ ." Read the nursery rhyme again, this time replacing the word *lassie* with *laddie*.

- What is this nursery rhyme about?
  - Partner Talk: What is this nursery rhyme about? (A girl who goes this way and that way.)
  - Listen for answers and paraphrase or repeat them back to the student to be sure you understand correctly. This serves as a model for students of how to listen and share ideas.
  - Have a student get up and model someone going "this way" and "that way" as you choral read the nursery rhyme for a third time.
  - Write "This way and that way" on chart paper and circle it. Tell the students you are going to work together to make a brainstorm web with ideas of why someone might be traveling different directions or with no clear path.
    - ▸ Give the students time to brainstorm or think about the question by themselves (a minute or so should be plenty of time).
    - ▸ Partner Talk: Why might a person travel without a clear path, going this way and that way and this way and that way?
    - ▸ Let each partner group share, adding to the ideas on the brainstorm web.

EDUCATOR'S TOOLBOX

Introduction

- Read the STEAM challenge card aloud to the class (see Appendix).
- Ask students to brainstorm what they might need to know about Lassie's city before they can help Lassie find her way home. Ideas they might mention are roads, buildings, the location of her home, and her current location. Share with students that all of those things can be found on a map.

- Share a map of your city with the students. You might want to use a smart board or a device to show an interactive map the students can manipulate to zoom in and out to examine features, like Google Maps.
- Explain to the students that today's challenge asks them to be civil engineers. Tell them a civil engineer is a special engineer who designs, creates, and maintains roads, bridges, tunnels, and buildings.
- As civil engineers, they will be required to use their "engineer eyes" to make observations or notice patterns. You can share this lesson's curiosity catchphrase here by saying: *I notice a pattern. Every river in the city has a bridge over it.* Encourage students to share observations like this that they notice.
- Point out relative location words they use and model a few more, if needed.
- Ask students also to wear their "engineer ears" to listen for friends using relative location or navigation words, like *right*, *left*, *beside*, *behind*, *next to*, *inside*, *near*, and *between*.

Investigation Procedure

1. Give each group a copy of Handout 2.1: Student's Toolbox to guide the investigation.
2. Give each group a foam board or a piece of cardboard to use as its city map. The students should begin by designating a starting point near the top of the board. Then they will choose an end point (Lassie's home) near the end of their board.
3. Next, students should brainstorm common locations you might find in any city and add them to their map board. Examples of locations might be schools, libraries, grocery stores, gas stations, and fire and police stations. They can sketch these directly on the board or cut them out of construction paper and paste or tape them onto the board.
4. Students can then add in natural landform details reflective of the city Lassie is lost in. These might include rivers, lakes, or caves. Up until this point, students may decide to move buildings or landforms into different locations. This is okay; they are still planning a model of their city. Tell them that new areas of cities are often planned on paper or scale models like this before they are constructed.
5. At this point, the city should be completely planned. Encourage students not to move or tear down buildings because this would be costly

for a city. On that same note, add that it would be difficult or impossible to change a natural landform or body of water. This increases the challenge and spatial reasoning skills needed for the remainder of the lesson.

6. Once each group has completed its map, the students are ready to brainstorm Lassie's path or roadway. Have groups use cut strips of construction paper or sentence strips to map out her path through the city. When the groups finish their plans, have them tape down their path plans to their board and lean it against the wall. From this point forward, you want their boards to be vertical (or close to vertical) so that students can explore how gravity affects Lassie's path.

7. At this point, gather students back into one group and tell them it's time for them to see the tools and materials they will use to construct their roads. Each group will get cardboard tubes, a Ping-Pong ball to represent Lassie, scissors, and tape. Have some aluminum foil available as an additional material for groups that prefer to create their own tubes or joints for their path. (*Note.* Remind the students that they will be using gravity as their force to move Lassie down her path, just like they learned in Exploration 1.)

8. Explore and create! Now is the time for students to grab their materials and tools and set out to construct their path design. As the teacher, your job is now to stand back, watch, and listen. Model today's catchphrase by sharing what you notice about their maps. Listen to their problems. Use prompts that make them push further to solve a problem: *I understand what you are saying. It is frustrating when the ball doesn't go into the next tube. Why do you think it might be stopping? Do you notice anything that you might be able to change or adjust to make the ball fit through the hole?*

9. Students will likely make several adjustments to their designs as they work to get their Lassie, or ball, from the beginning to the end. This should be encouraged. It means they are learning by changing their thinking.

10. If a group finishes early, have the group members tell you about the design, but more importantly, what they noticed and learned along the way as they explored. Ask students what they wonder now that they've completed one path for Lassie. They might wonder if they could create a path using fewer turns or only aluminum foil. Encourage them to test their wondering while other students are wrapping up their investigations.

Reflect

- Let the students do a Scientist Stroll to take a look at other groups' designs. Each group can leave out their ball for classmates to test their map and pathway.
- Have the students tell what they noticed using their "engineer eyes" about the various designs, looking for patterns. They might share ways their designs are alike and ways they are different.
- Tell the students you heard them use some of the relative location words you'd asked them to listen for with their "engineer ears" during their investigation. Repeat the vocabulary, if needed. If students are unable to share many examples, model some for them using their design boards: *I notice you have the cardboard tube going over the water. I see the police station is above the hospital on your map.*
- Tell students that civil engineers use these words when they are using a skill called *spatial reasoning* (or spatial visualization) to design and plan a city. Say: *This is a challenging skill that engineers practice for years. It is the ability to visualize, or see the town in your mind, and problem solve by helping Lassie move around things like buildings and other rivers. It's a challenge.* Let groups share some of the things they tried that didn't work and what they learned from those mistakes.
- Partner Talk: How is this similar to Exploration 1: Hickory, Dickory, Dock? (Both Lassie and the mice used gravity to get to their "homes.")

Wonder

- Ask the students to tell you what they wonder now that they've created a path for Lassie. Or in other words, what would they do if they had the opportunity to investigate this challenge again? Are there any additional materials they'd like to try? For example, a student might say, "I wonder if I could make a map that would work for a larger ball."
- Adding the materials for this lesson to your science center will give students the opportunity to test out their wonderings on another day.

Additional Literature Connections and Resources

Beaty, A. (2013). *Rosie Revere, engineer.* New York, NY: Abrams Books for Young Readers.

Rosie Revere is a young girl who dreams of becoming an engineer. She explores, problem solves, and learns from mistakes to refine her inventions.

Rabe, T. (2002). *There's a map on my lap!: All about maps.* New York, NY: Random House Books for Young Readers.

In this book, the Cat in the Hat introduces young readers to the various types and purposes of maps. He also shares interesting facts about locations featured in the text.

Spires, A. (2014). *The most magnificent thing.* Tonawanda, NY: Kids Can Press.

In *The Most Magnificent Thing*, a little girl and her dog set out to build the most magnificent thing! The little girl learns about perspective and perseverance as she creates.

STEAM

Name: _____ Date: _____

STUDENT'S TOOLBOX

👁	**ENGINEER EYES:** Watch what the ball is doing, notice problems, and look for solutions.
👂	**ENGINEER EARS:** Listen for your friends to say location words like *right*, *left*, *beside*, *behind*, *next to*, *inside*, *near*, and *between*.

1. Choose a Start location (near the top) and End or Home (near the bottom) for Lassie on your board.

2. Brainstorm buildings that might be in Lassie's city. Add them to your board.

3. Brainstorm natural locations (like rivers) and landforms you might find in Lassie's city. Add them to your board.

4. Check out your town and be sure you like the location of all of your places. After the next step, they can't be moved.

5. Plan a path for Lassie using sentence strips or paper. Remember to navigate around buildings and natural landforms in your town.

6. See your teacher for your surprise materials.

7. Play, create, and explore! Make mistakes, notice what you learned, and try again!

8. Keep going until you get Lassie to her home.

9. **Partner Talk:** How is Lassie's journey similar to the mice's journey in Hickory, Dickory, Dock? (*Hint*: Think about gravity.)

10. What did you learn?

11. What do you wonder now?

EXPLORATION 2: DID YOU EVER SEE A LASSIE?

WHAT'S HAPPENING IN THIS STEAM INVESTIGATION?

	Teacher	Student
Looks Like	- Moving around the room observing group work - Listening to student language, making notes of vocabulary or curiosity catchphrases used (nonevaluative)	- Exploring with materials, moving the cardboard tube path into different slopes and directions to get Lassie home - Listening to and watching other group members as they work together
Sounds Like	- Choral reading "Did You Ever See a Lassie?" - Modeling vocabulary and the curiosity catchphrase while observing group work - Asking questions to require students to dig deeper, make connections, or try again	- Choral reading "Did You Ever See a Lassie?" - Sharing observations using the "*I notice . . .*" curiosity catchphrase - Using relative location vocabulary while designing and creating the town - Sharing ideas, mistakes, and new learning

EXPLORATION

Hey Diddle Diddle: *Gravity and Actions/Reactions*

Hey diddle diddle,

The cat and the fiddle,

The cow jumped over the moon.

The little dog laughed,

To see such sport,

And the dish ran away with the spoon.

STEAM CHALLENGE

My goodness, that poor cow. He's out there jumping and jumping . . . and jumping. He just can't make it. But who can blame him? Have you ever tried to jump over the moon? Now the dog is laughing at him! Good thing the cow is friends with an engineer like you. Let's create a mini-trampoline and help that poor cow leap over the moon.

Goals and Objectives

During this exploration, students will:
- make observations to identify patterns in reactions,
- record "cow jump" data and observations, and
- learn to use appropriate lab safety equipment (e.g., goggles) to explore.

Materials

Note. Materials listed are needed per small group of students.
- Handout 3.1: Student's Toolbox
- Handout 3.2: Trampoline Test Data Collection Sheet
- Extra, extra large balloon (36–48 in.)*
- Bowl with 8–12-inch diameter
- Plastic toy cow or large rubber bouncy ball
- Masking tape
- Children's safety goggles
- Yardstick or ruler (optional)
- Crayons

*Don't have an extra, extra large balloon lying around the classroom? Don't throw out this activity! It can be done with a large balloon (12–18 in.) and a small plastic cup or bowl. You will want to adjust the size of your cow/ball, and the height of your moon in order to work best with the size of trampoline.

Important Investigation Ideas to Note

This investigation will give students the opportunity to delve deeper into Newton's laws of motion. Students will use the law of action-reaction to observe patterns and problem solve to help the cow jump over the moon.

- Newton's Third Law of Motion: For every action there is an opposite but equal reaction.
- Students will be looking for a pattern as they play and explore. They will notice that every time the cow is dropped on the trampoline, it bounces back in the air.
- The second pattern they will notice is the higher the cow is dropped, the higher the cow bounces. (Height and mass affect the gravitational potential energy of an object.) This observation will set the stage for a lesson the students will do later exploring potential and kinetic energy (see Exploration 4: Rock-a-Bye, Baby).
- The last idea to note that might help you answer any questions students have is the idea of "equal reaction." Students may believe, based on Newton's law, that the cow should come up to equal height of its starting point if there is an equal reaction. The reason why it does not is that some of the energy from the cow's fall creates the sound of it hitting the trampoline (sound is explored further in Exploration 7: Old King Cole), and some is converted to heat (remind them what they learned about friction in Exploration 1: Hickory, Dickory, Dock). The remainder of the energy is used in the cow's jump.

Language and Literacy

Curiosity Catchphrase

- *I notice . . .*

Vocabulary

- Height
- Gravity
- Action/Reaction

Speaking and Listening

- What is this nursery rhyme about?

- Read the poem aloud once to the students, then choral read the rhyme together as a class.
- Partner Talk: How do you think the cow feels about not being able to jump over the moon? (Sad, angry, embarrassed.)
- Let the students share their answers with the whole group. Students will likely connect to their own experiences with being unsuccessful at something or being laughed at. If students make connections, it might be a good time to model the catchphrase, *"This reminds me of . . ."*

- Why do you think the cow cannot jump over the moon?
  - Partner Talk: Why do you think the cow cannot jump over the moon?
  - Examples of discussion might include the following ideas: The moon is too high in the sky; the cow is too large to jump off of the ground very high; or it is impossible to jump to the sky—the cow would need a rocket.
  - Let several groups share their ideas.

EDUCATOR'S TOOLBOX

Introduction

Before the lesson, create the mini-trampoline. Cut the end off of the open end of the balloon. (This the part you would usually blow into.) Stretch the balloon over the bowl. Then cut out a moon from construction paper and tape it about one foot above the ground. You may need to adjust this measurement to work with your materials. Be sure to give it a test before you start with your students. Add height markers on the wall with masking tape.

- Tell the students that the cow heard all of their ideas as to why he couldn't jump over the moon, and he believes they can help him. Read the "Hey Diddle Diddle" challenge card to the students (see Appendix).
- Ask the students to think back to the mice racing down the ramp or Lassie making her way down the town map. Remind the students of the name of the force that pulls down toward the center of the Earth (gravity). Say: *If we know that the cow is having a problem jumping over*

the moon, how is gravity (the force that pulls us down toward the center of the Earth) making it hard for the cow to jump high?

- If needed, let them think independently and then partner talk about this question. Students will say that gravity is pulling the cow down, making it hard for him to jump really high.

- Tape a moon on the wall high enough that it would be difficult for a child to jump over. Ask for a student to come up and be the cow, demonstrating his problem. You might want to let several students (or all of the students) give it a shot.

- Ask the students if gravity pulled against them (yes) and how they knew. (They were pulled back down to the ground.) Say: *Unfortunately for the cow, we can't get rid of gravity. So, we need to be able to help the cow jump higher. Can anyone think of something that might be able to help you jump higher?*

- Brainstorm a list of ideas together. Sample ideas might be basketball shoes, moon shoes, a pogo stick, or a trampoline. (If no one says trampoline, you can add it to the list.) Tell the students that those are all great ideas, but today they are going to explore ways to help the cow jump using a trampoline. Tell them: *We will drop the cow from different heights to see if we can help the cow jump higher than the moon.*

- Ask the students what *height* means. If no one knows, tell them it means the distance from the ground and that in this lesson they are looking at the height of the fall and the height of the bounce or "jump."

- Put students in groups of two or three and assign them an area of the room against a wall or cabinet.

  • If you are working with older students or students at a higher level of readiness, you might want to give them a ruler, tape, and a moon, and let them create their own height measurement. You will have them start at the ground and put a strip of masking tape every 12 inches (or foot). They will mark 3 feet with their tape. Then they will tape the moon in between the first and second piece of tape (about 18 inches from the ground).

  • If you are working with younger students, they can use a nonstandard unit of measurement like a shoe or a piece of construction paper to measure where to put the tape, rather than a ruler. Or you might just choose to go ahead and have the tape markers and moons already taped to the wall for the students.

  • Any of these options will work fine. Do what is best for the needs and readiness levels of the little learners in your classroom.

Adjustments to Consider Based on Varied Materials

- It is important to note that the height the cow will bounce can change depending on the materials used to create the trampoline and the mass of the toy cow (or bouncy ball you may use to represent the cow). Remember to adjust the height of the moon to work best with your materials. You don't want the cow to succeed on the first jump—it isn't as exciting for the students. Be sure you test the measurements with your cow and trampoline and adjust accordingly. For example, if your cow bounces high, you might want to put your moon at 2 feet rather than 18 inches.

- The toy cow or the bouncy ball may not bounce straight up and down. The students might drop it at an angle. If you are using a plastic cow, it might hit headfirst and bounce back up at an angle. Encourage students to watch the cow at all times and wear their safety goggles.

- The students may need to move their trampoline to the left or right of the moon to get the cow to go over it. This is all a part of the problem solving.

Investigation Procedure

1. Give each group a trampoline (see Materials section for details) and a small plastic cow or a bouncy ball you are using to represent the cow. Also, give groups copies of Handout 3.1: Student's Toolbox to guide their investigation and Handout 3.2: Trampoline Test Data Collection Sheet to collect their observations. Students will record each jump in a different colored crayon (e.g., Jump 1 in red crayon, Jump 2 in a blue crayon, and Jump 3 in a green crayon).

2. Share and demonstrate with the students that they will drop (not throw) the cow from each of the height markers (or taped lines) in their area and record a drawing on Handout 3.2. Do at least one example with the whole class.

3. As you model, remind the students that you want them to watch with their "engineer eyes" for patterns. With their "engineer ears" they should hear the phrase, "*I notice . . .*" after each drop. The pattern you want them to notice is Newton's third law of motion: For every action, there is an opposite but equal reaction. In other words, every time the cow hits the trampoline, it bounces up in the air (action/reaction).

4. Each time the students drop the cow, they will drop it from a greater height marked by the tape. They may also notice the pattern that the greater the height it is dropped from, the greater the height of the bounce.

5. As the teacher, your job is now to stand back, watch, and listen. When invited by a group, you can play and explore with students, but you should be modeling the learning process, rather than knowing. For example, you might say: *I noticed that when you dropped the cow from the highest piece of tape, he went almost as high as the tape you dropped him from.*

6. Listen to students' problems. Ask questions that make them push further to solve a problem: *I understand it is frustrating that the cow keeps flying to the left of the moon. How can we move the trampoline to make the cow go over the moon?*

7. Remind students to record each test (draw in the height of the cow) on Handout 3.2.

8. If a group finishes early, have the group members not only tell you which height the cow was dropped from that allowed the cow to go "over the moon," but also share with you what they noticed, if they found a pattern, and what they wonder now.

Reflect

- On Handout 3.2, have the students circle the test or tests that allowed the cow to go over the moon.

- Let the students do a Scientist Stroll as a whole class, moving around the room to watch each group demonstrate its test that allowed the cow to travel over the moon.

- Call all of the students back to the whole-group area. Ask them to think back to their observations they made with their "engineer eyes and ears." Ask them to share if they noticed a pattern, or something that happened every time the cow was dropped or hit the trampoline. As previously stated, the students should have noticed that each time it hit the trampoline, the cow bounced.

- Tell the students that what they've observed was actually Isaac Newton's third law of motion. Tell them that for every action there is an opposite but equal reaction. Use the cow (ball) and trampoline to

model this as you say the words, or invite a student to show the example of the action and opposite but equal reaction.

- Partner Talk: Each time you dropped the cow from a greater height, what did you notice happened to the bounce? Students will share that they noticed the cow bounced higher from a greater height.

Wonder

- Ask the students to tell you what they wonder now that they've solved the cow's problem. For example, a student might say, "I wonder if we used something other than a balloon for the trampoline, would it still bounce the cow over the moon?"
- Adding the materials for this lesson to your science center will give students the opportunity to test out their wonderings on another day.
- If a student has not modeled the wondering, "I wonder why the bounce is greater from the higher tape," then model that wondering for the class. Tell students that they will explore that wondering in the next nursery rhyme challenge.

Additional Literature Connections and Resources

Christelow, E. (2012). *Five little monkeys jumping on the bed.* New York, NY: Houghton Mifflin Harcourt.

Five Little Monkeys Jumping on the Bed is a picture book of the traditional nursery rhyme. This book would offer students another opportunity to explore the concepts of action and reaction.

Robertson, W. C. (2002). *Force and motion: Stop faking it! Finally understanding science so you can teach it.* Arlington, VA: NSTA Press.

Force and Motion: Stop Faking It! Finally Understanding Science So You Can Teach It is a book for educators that helps you brush up on scientific concepts and theories before you teach.

STUDENT'S TOOLBOX

👁	**ENGINEER EYES:** What do you see happening to the cow every time it is dropped?
👂	**ENGINEER EARS:** Listen for your friends to say our physics words, like *gravity*, *action*, *reaction*, and *height*, and our curiosity catchphrase, "*I notice . . .*"

1. Check to be sure you have all of these materials: a plastic toy cow (or a ball to represent a cow), a trampoline, a moon taped to the wall, and three taped lines of different heights.

2. Investigate and test, dropping your cow from each of the three heights.

3. Record the height of each jump on Handout 3.2. Record Jump 1 in red crayon, Jump 2 in blue crayon, and Jump 3 in green crayon.

4. After each jump, use the catchphrase "*I notice . . .*" to help you look for a pattern of what happens every time you drop the cow.

5. **Partner/Group Talk:** What happens each time you drop the cow?

6. **Partner/Group Talk:** Which height was the best one to help the cow jump over the moon?

7. Circle the test on Handout 3.2 that shows which height, or heights, allowed the cow to jump over the moon.

8. **Partner Talk:** What happened to the cow's bounce when you dropped it from a higher location?

9. What do you wonder now?

EXPLORATION 3: HEY DIDDLE DIDDLE

TRAMPOLINE TEST DATA COLLECTION SHEET

Directions: Draw a picture of how high the cow jumped in each test. Record Jump 1 in red crayon, Jump 2 in blue crayon, and Jump 3 in green crayon.

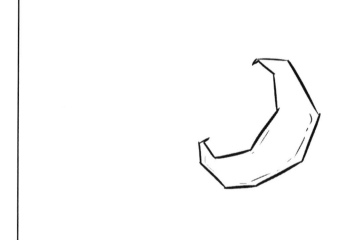

Height

Jump 1

EXPLORATION 3: HEY DIDDLE DIDDLE

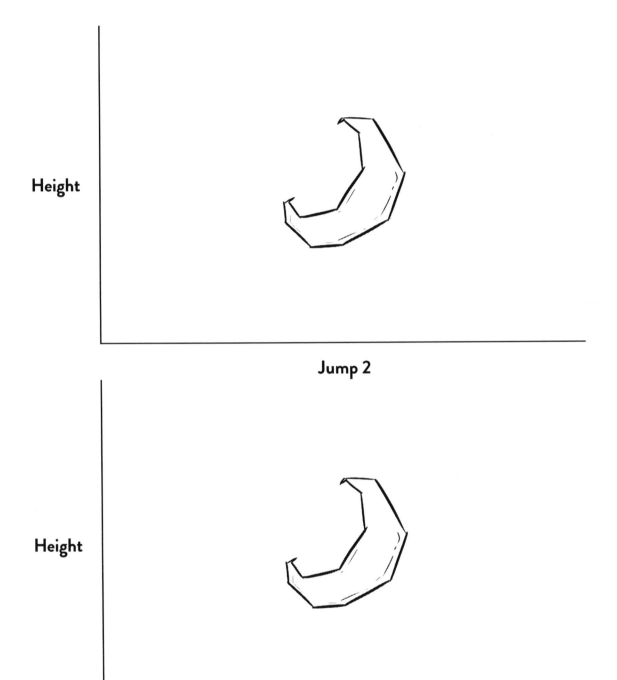

Height

Jump 2

Height

Jump 3

Circle the jump(s) that allowed the cow to jump *over* the moon.

Name: _____ Date: _____

WHAT'S HAPPENING IN THIS STEAM INVESTIGATION?

	Teacher	Student
Looks Like	- Moving around the room observing group work - Listening to student language, making notes of vocabulary or curiosity catchphrases used (nonevaluative)	- Wearing appropriate safety equipment - Testing different heights initially to get the cow to bounce higher than the moon - Listening to and watching other group members as they work together - Recording findings on Handout 3.2
Sounds Like	- Choral reading nursery rhyme - Modeling vocabulary and the curiosity catchphrase while observing group work - Asking questions to require students to dig deeper, make connections, or try again	- Choral reading nursery rhyme - Sharing observations using the "*I notice . . .*" curiosity catchphrase - Using vocabulary (*gravity*, *action*, *reaction*, and *height*) while testing, sharing, and recording findings - Sharing ideas, mistakes, and new learning

EXPLORATION 3: HEY DIDDLE DIDDLE

EXPLORATION 4

Rock-a-Bye, Baby: *Potential and Kinetic Energy*

Rock-a-bye, baby

In the treetop

When the wind blows

The cradle will rock

When the bough breaks

The cradle will fall

And down will come baby

Cradle and all.

STEAM CHALLENGE

This sweet baby loves to rock in her treetop, but she needs your help. The last time she fell asleep she was holding her bottle upside down and noticed it made the most interesting patterns on the ground while she was sleeping. She'd hoped to get a closer look, but unfortunately, the cradle broke, she fell on the accidental artwork, and now it's gone forever. Her parents have put her back in the cradle, she's holding her bottle over the side again just like last time, but she's having a string of bad luck. First the cradle breaks, and now there's no wind! The baby will not stop crying because she really wants to see her rocking milk artwork again. Her parents are in desperate need of an engineer and an artist to make some more beautiful cradle artwork for their daughter. Will you be a dear engineer and make some cradle artwork that doesn't depend on wind?

Goals and Objectives

During this exploration, students will:
- connect to schema or prior knowledge to solve problems,
- investigate energy in order to build schema, and
- create and describe pendulum artwork using STEAM vocabulary.

Materials

Note. The following materials may be used per small group of students or for a whole-class exploration.
- Handout 4.1: Student's Toolbox
- The cradle pendulum
  - Base: two sturdy objects (like chairs or suitcases)
  - Large stick or yardstick resting on top of the base
  - String

- Toy cradle (or video of a cradle rocking side to side)
- "Baby bottle" pendulum bob*
  - Water bottle with glue bottle top (an adult can hot glue the glue top to the water bottle)

- Hole punch
- Duct tape

- Large roll of paper (brown craft paper or bulletin board paper)
- Wet wipes
- Pendulum paint (1 part tempera paint to 1 part water)
- Children's safety goggles
- Gloves

*There are several great videos on the Internet of various ways to create the paint bob for the pendulum. Jim Noonan has an easy-to-follow video explaining how to prepare your bottle on Martha Stewart's website at http://www.marthastewart.com/894554/pendulum-painting.

Note. This can be a messy investigation, but it is well worth the cleanup. If you want to simplify this exploration (and control the mess), make only one pendulum and call students up to work with you individually, or in small groups, rather than have multiple groups swinging paint at the same time. Another idea is to take this exploration outside and use sidewalk paint. Also, let the students help with the cleanup! Being responsible is a part of being an engineer, too!

This would also be a wonderful STEAM investigation for families to create together as a part of an early childhood family event.

Important Investigation Ideas to Note

In Exploration 3: Hey Diddle Diddle, the class ended with the wondering question, "I wonder why the cow's bounce is greater from the higher tape?" One important idea that helps to answer this question is that the greater the distance the cow, or ball, is dropped, the more gravitational potential energy it has; therefore, the more kinetic energy it has when it hits the trampoline. As the students create art using the pendulum, they will be exploring potential and kinetic energy. Students will be using the curiosity catchphrase "*This reminds me of . . .*" in this exploration to help them make connections to experiences they've already had with pendulums. Both a cradle and a swing are examples of pendulums young students have most likely already experienced. They may also connect to what they have learned in previous lessons about

gravity pulling objects toward the ground. Making these connections will help students have a deeper understanding of this investigation.

Language and Literacy

Curiosity Catchphrase

- *This reminds me of . . .*

Vocabulary

- Energy—potential and kinetic
- Pendulum
- Curved lines
- Straight lines

Speaking and Listening

- What is this nursery rhyme about?
  - Read the poem once aloud to students and then sing or choral read it together.
  - Partner Talk: In this rhyme the baby is rocked by the wind until she falls. What causes the baby to fall? (The bough broke.) What do you think it means when the rhyme says that the bough breaks? What might cause the cradle to fall?
  - Remind the students that the word *lassie* is a synonym of the word *girl*. Tell them *bough* has almost the same meaning as another word, *branch*. Tell them a bough is often used to describe the largest branch on a tree.
  - Brainstorm words other than bough that could have been used in the rhyme. (Examples might include *branch* or *limb*.)

EDUCATOR'S TOOLBOX

Introduction

Balloon Mini-Lesson

- Remind the students of the wondering from the previous investigation: "I wonder why the cow bounced higher when it was dropped from a higher location." Say: *Let's think about that question for a minute. When we are jumping on a trampoline, we don't usually jump off of things but just jump on the trampoline, right? So, let's think of what else that activity might remind us of. When is a time you might jump off of something?*

- Listen for answers; they may think of jumping off of a couch or a bed. Encourage them to describe what jumping off of each surface feels like. A good example of this for students is jumping off the side of a pool versus jumping off of a diving board. The students may notice that they hit the water harder or go deeper into the pool when jumping from a higher location.

- Ask the students if they can remember the name of the force that pulls them down to the ground (gravity). If they don't remember the name of the word, tell them. Explain that the higher they are up from the ground, like the cow, the more potential energy they have. Say: *The word* potential *means the ability to do something in the future. So, if I say keep practicing your letter sounds because you have the potential to be a great reader, what does that mean? It means you have the future ability to read!*

- Tie a balloon (not helium-filled) to a string and hang it from a high location in the room to make a pendulum. Pull the balloon back until the string is nearly parallel to the floor. Say: *A scientist would say this balloon now has potential energy. I wonder what that means. What would happen if I let go?* Give the students time to think about this, and then listen to their answers while you are still holding the balloon. The students may say the balloon will fall, if they are connecting to the other investigations, or they may say that the balloon will swing, if they can see that it is like a playground swing. Ask: *Who is ready to find out?*

- Before you let go, say: *Let's watch this potential energy transform into kinetic energy. Kinetic energy means energy in motion.* Let go of the balloon and let students observe it swing. Tell the students this is called a pendulum.

- Demonstrate a second time. This time say the words *potential energy* when the balloon is at the highest point and *kinetic energy* when it is in motion.

- Share the catchphrase model, "*This reminds me of. . .*" For example, you could say: *This reminds me of a playground swing because once I pull it back it will continue to swing back and forth until it stops in the center, just like when I'm playing at recess.*

Cradle Mini-Lesson

- Bring out a toy cradle and pull the cradle back to one side, just as you did the balloon. Let the students practice telling you when it has potential energy and when it has kinetic energy. (If you do not have access to a toy cradle, you can show a short video clip of a cradle and let students watch it move.)
- Partner Talk: "This reminds me of a cradle because. . ." Students will model off of your example, discussing ways the balloon pendulum is like a cradle.
- Pull out the STEAM challenge card (see Appendix) and read it to the class. Say: *Lucky for the family, we are a class full of engineers and artists who understand how pendulums work. Are you ready to help the baby create artwork? The family says that the baby's bottle made artwork on the ground while she rocked to sleep. If we know how a pendulum moves, can someone make a prediction for what that artwork might have looked like?*
- Have students record their predictions on a piece of paper. The general idea here is that the lines of the artwork will mimic the back and forth motion of the cradle pendulum, but please remember this is just a prediction. It is perfectly fine if the prediction does not look like the end result. When the prediction is different from the final result, this is evidence of learning.

Investigation Procedure

1. You may want to move outside for this activity or cover the students' work area in drop cloths. See Materials list for tips on setting up each pendulum.
2. Each student will create his or her own artwork; however, the students can work in small groups, taking turns using the pendulum(s) you create. (*Note.* You do not have to create one pendulum per group unless you wish to do so. If you are working with very young students, you might choose to make one pendulum for the class and work with students in small groups for this investigation.)
3. You might want to do one demonstration of steps 4–7 for the class before having them work in small groups to make their artwork. Give each group copies of Handout 4.1: Student's Toolbox to guide its investigation.

4. Place a sheet of paper under the pendulum. Have the students put on goggles and gloves and then choose the height at which they will drop the pendulum. Students will test the pendulum one at a time. Before they let go of the pendulum, they can tell their friends that the bottle now has potential energy; when it is swinging, they can practice identifying kinetic energy. Then when it reaches the highest point on the other side, they can note its potential energy again. They do not need to continue naming this pattern unless they choose to do so.

5. After explaining how the pendulum is moving using their vocabulary, they might like to chant the "Rock-a-Bye, Baby" nursery rhyme until the pendulum stops moving.

6. Once the paint bottle bob is at rest, demonstrate how to put one finger over the hole to stop the flow of paint. Alternatively, students can twist the glue top closed to stop the flow of paint.

7. The student (or an adult) can carefully pick up the sheet of paper and move it to a spot to dry.

8. The next student can lay his or her paper under the pendulum, put a finger over the hole in the bottle, pull the bottle back to the height of his or her choosing, and repeat steps 4–7. Continue with this pattern until all of the students have had a turn.

9. Remind the students that as they watch their classmates explore and create, they can describe what they see happening using their catchphrase from today, "*This reminds me of . . .*"

10. As the teacher, your job is now to stand back, watch, and listen. Model today's catchphrase by sharing real-world connections to pendulums or students' artwork. Listen to their problems. Ask questions that make them push further to solve a problem: *It is disappointing when the paint goes off of the paper. How could you make it have a smaller path?*

11. You might also want to model the vocabulary of *curved lines* and *straight lines* as you walk around and discuss students' artwork.

12. If a group finishes early, have its members tell you not only about the design of their artwork, but also what they noticed and learned along the way. Ask them to share what they learned about creating pendulum artwork and what patterns they might have noticed. Let them share what they wonder now that they know how to help the baby make a pendulum painting.

Reflect

- Let the students do a Scientist Stroll to take a look at their classmates' designs.
- Revisit the bottle pendulum prediction pattern from the cradle mini-lesson and compare it to one of the pendulum paintings created by a student in your class. Let the students share differences and similarities they notice.
- Partner Talk: Do you think the baby and her family will be happy with the bottle pendulum artwork you made for her?
- After the artwork has dried, let the students show you the point in the drawing that the pendulum had the potential energy (the farthest point on the curved outer ends) and the lines of motion that show the pendulum's kinetic energy.
- Ask the students to share examples of things they heard friends share during the investigation, using the phrase *"This reminds me of . . ."*

Wonder

- Ask the students to tell you what they wonder now that they have created this artwork for the baby. Or in other words, what would they do if they had the opportunity to investigate this challenge again? Are there any additional materials they'd like to try? For example, a student might say, "I wonder if I could make a pendulum using LEGOs and a ball."
- Adding the materials for this lesson to your science center will give students the opportunity to test out their wonderings on another day.

Additional Literature Connections and Resources

Bradley, K. B. (2010). *Energy makes things happen*. New York, NY: Harper Collins.

   Energy Makes Things Happen is a picture book that explains the concept of energy and how it is used.

Robertson, W. C. (2002). *Energy: Stop faking it! Finally understanding science so you can teach it*. Arlington, VA: NSTA Press.

   This book helps educators brush up on scientific concepts and theories before they present them to their classes.

Name: _____ Date: _____

STUDENT'S TOOLBOX

ENGINEER EYES:
Watch the pendulum's movement and notice patterns.

ENGINEER EARS:
Listen for your friends to say engineer words like *energy*, *potential energy*, *kinetic energy*, *gravity*, *pendulum*, *curved lines*, and *straight lines*, and make connections to what they already know by using today's catchphrase, "*This reminds me of . . .*"

1. All group members need to put on their safety goggles and gloves.

2. Put your finger over the hole in the bottle that is leaking paint and move your pendulum.

3. Place your paper underneath the pendulum.

4. Now it's time to play and create!

5. Pull the bottle back to give it the amount of potential energy you want it to have. Release it, watching the potential energy transform to kinetic energy as it swings.

6. Your group might even want to chant the "Rock-a-Bye, Baby" rhyme as you watch the pendulum create your art.

7. When the pendulum stops, put a finger back over the hole to stop the paint from flowing and move the pendulum out of the way.

EXPLORATION 4: ROCK-A-BYE, BABY

8. Pick up your artwork and move it to the drying area. *Tip*: Wet wipes are at your center, if your hands get dirty.

9. As the rest of your group members create their artwork, be sure to chant the rhyme with them and share what you notice. Challenge yourself to use those new energy words!

10. **Partner Talk:** This artwork reminds me of . . .

11. **Partner Talk:** How are our designs alike? How are they different?

12. Now that you know how to make a paint pendulum, what do you wonder?

STEAM

WHAT'S HAPPENING IN THIS STEAM INVESTIGATION?

	Teacher	Student
Looks Like	- Moving around the room observing group work - Listening to student language, making notes of vocabulary or curiosity catchphrases used (nonevaluative)	- Wearing appropriate safety equipment - Exploring with the pendulum, pulling it back and releasing it to make artwork - Listening to and watching other group members as they work together
Sounds Like	- Choral reading "Rock-a-Bye, Baby" - Modeling vocabulary and the curiosity catchphrase while observing group work - Asking questions to require students to dig deeper, make connections, or try again	- Choral reading "Rock-a-Bye, Baby" - Sharing observations using the curiosity catchphrase "*This reminds me of . . .*" - Using vocabulary (*potential energy, kinetic energy, gravity, curved lines, straight lines,* and *pendulum*) while creating artwork - Sharing ideas, mistakes, and new learning with teacher and classmates

EXPLORATION 4: ROCK-A-BYE, BABY

EXPLORATION

5

Miss Mary Mack: *Simple Machines*

Miss Mary Mack, Mack, Mack

All dressed in black, black, black

With silver buttons, buttons, buttons

All down her back, back, back

She asked her mother, mother, mother

For fifty cents, cents, cents

To watch the elephant, elephant, elephant

Jump over the fence, fence, fence

. . . continues on the next page

. . . *continued.*

He jumped so high, high, high

That he reached the sky, sky, sky

And he didn't come back, back, back

Until the Fourth of July, 'ly, 'ly!

STEAM CHALLENGE

The circus is in an uproar. The number one attraction, the fence-jumping elephant, Mr. Eli, had one too many peanuts at the last stop and can't make the jump! No one wants the beloved elephant to get hurt, and the ringmaster is threatening to cancel the show, but Mr. Eli is determined nothing will stop him from jumping the fence. His dear friend, Mary Mack, is all dressed up and has borrowed money from her mother to see the show. He does not want to let her down. Mr. Eli has heard that you are an engineer and wondered if you could design a contraption to help him leap over the fence. So, what do you say? Are you willing to help Mr. Eli?

Goals and Objectives

During this exploration, students will:
- make predictions and inferences by using the phrase *"I think if . . .",*
- create a simple lever to catapult an elephant or cotton ball, and
- reflect on observations to determine the most effective catapult materials and design.

Materials

Note. Materials listed are needed per small group of students.
- Handout 5.1: Student's Toolbox
- Handout 5.2: Elephant Catapult Recording Sheet
- Children's safety goggles

- Scissors
- Gray cotton ball or pom-pom (to serve as the elephant)
- Blocks (stacked to desired height to serve as the fence)
- Large popsicle stick with a bottle cap glued to one end (arm of lever)
- Various-sized cylinders: corks, glue sticks, marker caps (fulcrum)
- Picture or video of a seesaw
- Whole-group demonstration supplies for larger catapult
  - Small plastic elephant
  - Piece of wood: suggested size 5 1/2 in. x 36 in. (arm of lever)
  - Wooden cylinder block or coffee can (fulcrum)

Important Investigation Ideas to Note

Students will create a catapult by exploring class 1 levers in this investigation. The students will build on the previous challenge experiences and their understanding of the laws of force and motion, as well as potential and kinetic energy, to help the elephant "jump" over the fence. The students will see that levers, like all simple machines, make doing work easier by reducing the amount of force needed to complete a task. Did you know there is a formula for work in physics?

$$Work = Force \times Distance$$

Levers are simple machines made up of the following basic parts: arm (beam), fulcrum, force, and load. Levers that students may have seen in the real world include seesaws, hammer claws, and oars. Scissors and pliers are made of two class 1 levers.

Language and Literacy

Curiosity Catchphrase

- *I think if . . .*

Vocabulary

- Lever
- Simple machines

- Catapult
- Force

Speaking and Listening

- Nursery rhyme repetition
  - Chant the poem once, clapping the rhythm, and then have students do it with you the second time you read it.
  - Tell the students this poem uses a writing technique called *repetition*.
  - What does repetition mean? (Note the root word *repeat*, if needed.)
  - Partner Talk: Why do you think authors would use repetition? (To create rhythm or make an idea stand out to the reader.)

- What is this nursery rhyme about?
  - The rhyme is about Miss Mary Mack and a special event.
  - Partner Talk: What lines in the poem help us see that this event, the elephant jumping over the fence, is very special to Mary Mack? (She is dressed up, wearing silver buttons, and has borrowed money from her mother.)

EDUCATOR'S TOOLBOX

Introduction

- After reading and discussing the poem together, ask if anyone has a prediction of what the challenge today might be. Then, take out the STEAM challenge card (see Appendix) and read it to the students.
- Pull out a toy elephant, the wooden board, and the cylinder you are using for your fulcrum. Bring over an empty student chair. Tell the students you will pretend the chair is a fence that the elephant must jump over. Say: *You are going to play, explore, and investigate, and by the end of this lesson, we will use these materials to launch the elephant over the fence!*
- Tell the students that because there is only one elephant, they will conduct their investigation by exploring on similar, but smaller, materials. Share the materials with them: the craft sticks with bottle caps on

top, the fulcrum options (marker tops, glue sticks, corks), and the gray pom-poms that will represent the elephants.

- Show students the coffee can and smaller fulcrum options and ask them to notice the 3-D shape of all of the objects, both large and small (cylinder). Also, show them their safety goggles and have them tell you why safety goggles are needed in this experiment. (The elephants, or pom-poms, will be flying!)

- Show students a pair of scissors. Ask them to focus on only one of the beams, or arms. (The pair of scissors is made of two class 1 levers put together, so we only want them to watch one part at a time for this demonstration.) Show them how when you lift one handle of the scissors, the blade goes down. Ask them to notice what happens when the blade goes down (the handle goes up).

- Show the students a picture (or video) of a seesaw and describe how when one child goes down the other goes up. Ask them to tell you what they think happens when the other child goes back down? (The first child goes up.)

- Partner Talk: How are the seesaw and scissors alike? (When one part is lifted, the other goes down, and vice versa.)

- Show the seesaw again. Point out the arm, or beam, and the fulcrum on the seesaw. Tell the students this is a simple machine called a *lever*. Say: *Levers help us do work, and today they will help do the work to get the elephant over the fence.* Show students that their fence will be a stack of blocks.

- Tell them this investigation has a couple of guidelines:
  1. The only object that is allowed to fly through the air is the gray pom-pom.
  2. They must wear their safety goggles at all times.

Investigation Procedure

1. Tell students: *A catapult is an invention that is used to launch something in the air. Today we will use what we've learned about levers to create a catapult to help Mr. Eli the Elephant. How do you think we can use this beam* (hold up the craft stick) *and one of these fulcrums* (hold up cylinders like corks, marker caps, and glue sticks) *to make our elephants* (hold up the gray pom-poms) *jump over the fence?* Let them discuss ideas with a

partner. Students may mention using the beam like a bat; remind them they have to use all three parts: the craft stick, cylinder, and pom-pom.

2. Introduce the catchphrase "*I think if . . .*" to the students by modeling some of the ideas you hear them share in the partner talk. For example: "I think if we put the glue stick under the craft stick, it will work like a seesaw." Tell them this catchphrase helps them learn to plan and share ideas.

3. Say: *Now that you've learned a little about levers, you are ready to play and investigate to help us learn how to get Mr. Eli the Elephant over the fence. Remember you are going to explore with your smaller materials, and at the end of the class we will make a plan to get our larger elephant over the fence (or the chair).*

4. Have students work in partners or small groups to come up with their first "*I think if . . .*" statement that will help them get started with the investigation. For example: "I think if we put the cotton ball in the cap on the craft stick, it will help the elephant hold still while we launch it."

5. Distribute materials and copies of Handout 5.1: Student's Toolbox. Then have students play, explore, and investigate. Students will try things that do not work. As long as they are following the safety rules, this is okay. If students are stuck, or having a hard time getting the elephant to fly, you can encourage them to take a Scientist Stroll around the classroom to scout and learn from others' ideas. Once they have done this, have them share with you an "*I think if . . .*" plan and get back to exploring.

6. As you walk around, help students understand how forces play an important role in this investigation. The students input force on one side of the lever to make the pom-pom fly. Gravity pulls the pom-pom back to the ground.

7. If students finish early, give them more blocks and ask them to do another test to try to get the elephant over a higher fence.

8. As students finish, have them clean up the materials and then give them copies of Handout 5.2: Elephant Catapult Recording Sheet. Tell the students to reflect or remember back to what method worked the best for them to get the elephant over the fence. Ask them to draw a picture or diagram that shares how they believe the class should create the lever to catapult the elephant over the chair.

Reflect

- Partner Talk: Share your illustration with your friend and explain why you believe this is the best design. (Share several of these with the class.)
- Have the students notice common design elements in each illustration shared. Use these elements to create one design plan sketch for the class to test on the board or a large piece of paper.
- Build the lever and catapult and test the design. If it does not work, let students refine the design and try again.
- Ask students if they believe they successfully solved Mr. Eli's problem in this challenge. Ask them how they know they did (or did not) succeed in this mission.
- Tell the students: *The end of the poem states that the elephant reached the sky and didn't come back until July 4th. What do you know about gravity? Would it really be possible for an elephant to stay up in the air that long? Why or why not?*

Wonder

- Ask the students to tell you what they wonder now that they've designed, created, and tested this catapult. For example: "We made a catapult that launched the elephant over the chair; now I'm wondering if we can create a catapult that will launch the elephant over the shelf."
- Adding the materials for this lesson to your science center will give students the opportunity to test out these wonderings on another day.

Additional Literature Connections and Resources

Macaulay, D. (2015). *How machines work: Zoo break!* New York, NY: DK Children.
    This book uses engaging illustrations and models to explain the functions of six simple machines: levers, pulleys, screws, inclined planes, wedges, and wheels.

Wells, R. E. (1996). *How do you lift a lion?* Morton Grove, IL: Whitman.
    How Do You Lift a Lion? is picture book that shares a basic introduction to levers, wheels, and pulleys.

STUDENT'S TOOLBOX

> 👁 **ENGINEER EYES:**
> Watch how levers/catapults work. What patterns do you see?
>
> 👂 **ENGINEER EARS:**
> Listen for friends to share ideas using engineer words like *lever*, *simple machine*, *catapult*, and *force*, and today's catchphrase, "*I think if . . .*"

1. Welcome to the circus! Mr. Eli the Elephant needs your help! Build a fence using your blocks.

2. **Think about your materials:** How can they be used to create a catapult to launch the elephant over the fence, or the stack of blocks?

3. **Partner Talk:** Use the catchphrase "*I think if . . .*" to help you plan and share your design plan (e.g., "I think if I put a marker cap under the craft stick, it will work like a seesaw.")

4. Make a plan for the materials each person in your group will need.

5. Gather your materials. Be sure to wear your safety goggles when you test your catapult.

6. Design, create, and investigate!

7. Use the catchphrase "*I think if . . .*" as you problem solve and plan.

8. If you are still stuck, do a Scientist Stroll, scouting to observe other groups working on the investigation, to learn something new.

9. Remember you are exploring to help our class work together to solve this challenge at the end of our lesson.

10. When you have finished, clean up, and draw a picture on Handout 5.2 of how you think we should make our catapult to get the elephant over the fence.

11. What do you wonder now? How could you innovate to make your design even better?

ELEPHANT CATAPULT RECORDING SHEET

Name: _____   Date: _____

Directions: Draw a picture of the catapult you created to help the elephant "jump" over the fence.

Name: _____ Date: _____

WHAT'S HAPPENING IN THIS STEAM INVESTIGATION?

	Teacher	Student
Looks Like	- Moving around the room observing group work - Listening to student language, making notes of vocabulary or curiosity catchphrases used (nonevaluative)	- Wearing appropriate safety equipment - Planning, designing, creating, and testing the catapult - Listening to and watching classmates or partners while working alongside them and during partner talks
Sounds Like	- Choral reading "Miss Mary Mack" - Modeling vocabulary and the curiosity catchphrase while observing group work - Asking questions to require students to dig deeper, make connections, or try again	- Choral reading "Miss Mary Mack" - Sharing curiosity and planning using the catchphrase "I think if . . ." - Using vocabulary (lever, catapult, simple machine, force) while designing and creating - Sharing ideas, mistakes, and new learning with teacher and classmates

EXPLORATION 5: MISS MARY MACK

EXPLORATION

6

London Bridge: *Engineering*

London Bridge is falling down,
Falling down, falling down.
London Bridge is falling down,
My fair lady.

STEAM CHALLENGE

The bridge is falling down . . . falling down! Who wants to be on a bridge that is falling down? No one! *The Daily Times* reported that the bridge fell while a truck full of apples from the local orchard was crossing it. Don't worry. No one was hurt, but the city is desperate to make a plan for a new bridge that will not fall with a truck full of apples . . . or a car full of people! Thankfully, the city has architects and engineers like you to solve this problem. Design and create a new model of a bridge strong enough to hold nine apples to help your friends in London learn how to make a stronger bridge.

Goals and Objectives

During this exploration, students will:
- recognize mistakes and communicate new learning related to those mistakes;
- design, create, and test a bridge to determine if it will hold nine apples; and
- record and share observations from the bridge test.

Materials

Note. Materials listed are needed per small group of students. Students do not have to use all of these materials.
- Handout 6.1: Student's Toolbox
- Handout 6.2: London Bridge Recording Sheet
- Photographs or pictures of bridges
- Cardboard tubes
- Small wooden blocks and/or small wood rounds
- Craft sticks
- Aluminum foil
- Masking tape
- String
- Binder clips, plastic clamps, or clothespins
- Scissors
- Blue or green paper (cut to model the river)

- Paper clips
- 1-liter bottle of water
- 9 small or medium-sized apples
- 2 identical buckets or bags

Important Investigation Ideas to Note

In this challenge, students will explore the concepts of mass, measurement, and weight. In previous lessons, the students investigated using the force of gravity. This lesson will build on those experiences, but now they will begin to understand the idea that weight is a force. *Weight* and *mass* are often used as synonyms in early childhood, but the two words have different meanings. Weight is the force generated by gravity on an object and can be changed based on your location. Mass is a physical property of an object and will not change based on location. The most common example of this concept is that your weight will be different on the moon than on Earth; however, your mass will be the same. Students are *not* expected to fully understand this concept at the end of this lesson. This information is provided as background information for you, the teacher, to help you plan and facilitate this investigation.

The students will also become architects and engineers in this exploration as they plan and design their bridges. The lesson begins by looking at photographs of bridges, hunting for common shapes. The students should notice that the triangle is a shape that appears over and over again in many different bridges. Triangles have the ability to hold their shape and remain strong in designs because added force, or weight, is distributed throughout the shape. This lesson will give students the opportunity to explore using triangles and their function in architectural structures.

Language and Literacy

Curiosity Catchphrase

- *Oops, I learned . . .*

Vocabulary

- Bridge—arch, truss, beam, suspension
- Shapes—triangle, rectangle, circle (two-dimensional)

- Heavy
- Light

Speaking and Listening

- What is this nursery rhyme about?
  - Choral read the poem together as a class.
  - Partner Talk: What might cause a bridge to fall down?
  - Partner Talk: What sort of problems might a city have if its bridge is out?
  - There are many possible answers to these two questions. Remember that at this point none of them are right or wrong. These open-ended questions offer a good opportunity to let students know that every idea shared is valued and respected.

EDUCATOR'S TOOLBOX

Introduction

Before you begin the lesson, build a very simple, weak bridge that you will use for the students' investigation. Use the same materials to build your bridge that the students will have access to in this investigation. (*Note.* You want this bridge to hold fewer than nine apples.)

- Choral read the poem again, but this time ask the students to listen for a problem they can help solve with their "engineer ears." Ask if anyone can predict the challenge for the day. Pull out the STEAM challenge card (see Appendix) and read it to the students.
- Tell the students you have a model of the bridge from the poem and will demonstrate for them what happened. You will be using apples to apply weight to your bridge to test the strength. Ask the students to watch what happens with "engineer eyes."
- Let the students add one apple at a time until the bridge breaks. (There is often a lot of joy or sorrow at watching things break, even in science. This is great; it means the students are engaged.)
- Introduce the catchphrase "*Oops, I learned . . .*" Tell the students that sometimes we learn more from the breaks and mistakes than when things go right. Ask them to describe for you what they noticed and

what they can learn from it. Students learn quite a bit from the break. It helps them understand and find the weak spots in the bridge design. This lesson will prove that mistakes are an important part of learning.

- If needed you can model for the students: *Oops, the bridge broke. I learned that this design is only strong enough to hold three apples.* Or: *Oops, the bridge broke! I learned that it needs more support in the center if I want it to hold more apples.*

- Tell the students that mistakes and accidents are an opportunity to learn and that you expect them to make mistakes today. You may even want to let them share mistakes they have made in previous lessons and what they learned from them.

- Say: *Today you will be a structural engineer, a special type of civil engineer who helps make sure structures are safe by understanding how sturdy they are and how much weight they can hold. Your challenge will be to design a bridge that holds nine apples.*

  - Tell the students that one liter of water weighs about one kilogram, and a bag of nine small- to medium-sized apples, like the one you are using, weighs about 2 kilograms.

  - Share with students that a paper clip weighs about one gram, and because *kilo* means 1,000, this means that 1,000 paper clips would weigh one kilogram. Tell them a bottle of water weighs about one kilogram.

- Have a student come up to the front of the room and hold her arms out straight, like a human balance. This pose might remind students of a seesaw or the lever they created in Exploration 5. Put a paper clip in one bucket and a one-liter bottle of water in the other. Put a bucket in each hand and have the student keep her arms out straight. Have her drop the heavier bucket closer to the ground and lift the lighter bucket higher up. This lets the student feel and share with her classmates the difference in weight between one paper clip, about 1 gram, and one liter of water, about 1 kilogram.

- Next, have a student compare nine apples to one liter of water. In one hand put a bag or bucket with one liter of water (about 1 kg), and in the other hand put a bucket with nine apples (about 2 kg).

- Encourage students to describe the difference in the two buckets. Encourage them to use the words *heavier* or *heavy* and *lighter* or *light* in their description. You can let several students come up to feel and

describe the difference. The descriptions may be repetitive, but that is okay. Repetition is how they learn to own new words.

- Tell the students that now that they know their task (to design a bridge) and the goal (to design a bridge that holds nine apples, or about 2 kg), they are ready to start problem solving with their friends. Explain to the students that this investigation will require them to work together like architects and civil engineers. The students might remember from the Lassie investigation that civil engineers design bridges. Share with them that architects are also involved in designing bridges and work closely with the engineers. Both architects and engineers would have learned from observing mistakes in the bridge that broke, but they would also do research and look at examples of other bridges.

- Share photographs of various types of bridges with the class. Pass them around to the students. When possible, pull examples from your town or state. Beam bridges are found in almost every area. They are often seen in places like overpasses and over short distances of water. A few popular examples of other types of bridges include the following:
  - Arch bridge: Sydney Harbor Bridge, New River Gorge Bridge
  - Truss bridge: Betsy Ross Bridge
  - Suspension bridge: Golden Gate Bridge

- Partner Talk: What shapes do we see most commonly in bridges?
- Partner Talk: Where do we see those shapes most often?
- You want to be sure that students notice that triangles are a common shape in bridges and are most often seen in the supporting structures of the bridge. They may also notice arches, lines, and pillars. Be sure they notice the location for these structures also.

Investigation Procedure

1. Put the students in small groups and give each group a "river" cut from construction paper.
2. Before they begin the investigation, remind students of today's catchphrase, "*Oops, I learned . . .*" Let them know that you are expecting them to make a mistake today and tell you what they've learned from it.
3. Distribute Handout 6.1: Student's Toolbox and Handout 6.2: London Bridge Recording Sheet. Have each group determine the type of bridge it will make and circle the shapes to be used in the bridge.

4. Show students the materials that will be available to them and have them talk with their group about what materials they may need to build their bridge.

5. Have the students bring their plan to you and request materials. They can collect their materials in a tray (chip and dip trays are great for sorting materials) and take them back to their area. As they "shop" for their materials, remind them that the class will share all available materials. So, if they take all of the plastic clamps and string, no other group will have the opportunity to use them. (*Note.* Students do not have to use all available materials. You can build a bridge with only one or two items.)

6. Sometimes, with investigations like this one, we choose to give students the materials they need and then move on with the investigation. However, we want to be sure that in some explorations we give students the opportunities to plan and make choices about the materials they use, as suggested in this lesson. Planning is one of the most challenging parts of an investigation. Requiring students to plan and make choices for the materials they will need, even if they end up needing something different in the end, boosts the level of challenge.

7. If you are working with younger students and feel it may be difficult for them to manage five or six materials, you can limit the number of materials they use to two or three. You can make a bridge with only foil and wooden blocks or craft sticks and tape. Find a way to manage (and control) the process that still allows the students to plan and make choices.

8. Then let the students go create and build their bridge! They may want to test as they go along. If they want to build a portion and do a mini-test to see how the bridge does with a couple of apples or one bottle of water, encourage them to do that.

9. The bridge may break as they are building or doing the mini-test listed; remind them this is okay. Mistakes are how we learn. Invite them to use the catchphrase "*Oops, I learned . . .*"

10. Students may request different materials than what they previously asked for. This is an example of them learning to analyze and modify their thinking into new ideas, which requires a higher level of thinking.

11. After the bridge is designed, have them draw an illustration on Handout 6.2 of what the bridge looks like before the test. If a group finishes early, have its members tell you not only about the design of

their bridge, but also what mistakes they've made and learned along the way. Let them share what they wonder now that they know how to do this activity.

12. The test: You can do the test as a whole group or in small groups. Doing the test as a whole group allows for the students to really take a close look at each group's design and learn from others. Let each member of the group add one apple at a time until the bridge fails, or until it successfully holds all nine apples.

13. Have each student draw an illustration to show what happened during the test.

Reflect

- Let students share their drawings and what they learned about the bridges they built with members of different groups.

- The catchphrase "*Oops, I learned . . .*" will provide a good reflection sentence starter for a group that had a bridge that failed. If a group's bridge didn't fail, they could still use this catchphrase by noticing weak points as they tested. For example, if the deck started to bow with the apples, they might say, "Oops, the bridge bent when it held nine apples. I learned that I need to add another block to the center."

- As in previous lessons, have students share their partners' ideas rather than their own with the class. This encourages them to listen and respect others' thoughts and ideas.

- Partner Talk: How would our model help London learn to build a stronger bridge?

Wonder

- Ask the students to tell you what they wonder now that they've designed, created, and tested this bridge for London. They might say something like, "I didn't use string in this design. I wonder if I could make a suspension bridge that would hold nine apples."

- Adding the materials for this lesson in your block or science center will give students the opportunity to test out their wonderings on another day.

Additional Literature Connections and Resources

Beaty, A. (2007). *Iggy Peck, architect*. New York, NY: Abrams Books for Young Readers.

Iggy Peck is a creative kid-architect who loves to construct things out of unique materials.

Bunting, E. (2006). *Pop's bridge*. New York, NY: HMH Books for Young Readers.

Robert's father is building the Golden Gate Bridge, and he couldn't be more proud! This story tells the account of one young boy and his father in the construction of this beautiful bridge.

Macaulay, D. (2004). *Building big*. New York, NY: HMH Books for Young Readers.

Building Big shares information on how and why structures are designed and created, and challenges that must be overcome in engineering and architecture.

Saltzberg, B. (2010). *Beautiful oops!* New York, NY: Workman.

This book uses art to teach the important concept of learning from mistakes. A spill can become a hopping frog, and bent paper might be the beginning of a penguin. With imagination and observation, mistakes are just an opportunity to make something better.

STUDENT'S TOOLBOX

👁 **ENGINEER EYES:**
Notice shapes in other bridges. Watch for bowing or bending.

👂 **ENGINEER EARS:**
Listen for your friends to say architecture and engineering words, like *heavy, light, shapes, rectangle, triangle, circle, arches,* and *lines,* and our catchphrase, *"Oops, I learned . . ."*

1. Lay your river down on the ground. You will build your bridge over this river.

2. **Partner Talk:** What type of bridge will you create?

3. **Partner Talk:** What shapes will you use to create your bridge? (Remember to think back to the shapes in the photos we looked at.) Circle those shapes on Handout 6.2.

4. Take a look at the materials that you can use.

5. **Partner Talk:** Decide which materials you will use to create your bridge.

6. Gather materials. (Your teacher will tell you how to do this.)

7. Design, create, and investigate!

8. **Mini-Test:** You may choose to do a mini-test as you create. This means you will test your design using a few apples to decide if you are happy with your design.

9. Remember that you will try things that fail today! That just means you are learning. Say, "*Oops, I learned . . .*" and clean up and carry on!

10. When you have finished your design and are ready to test it, draw a picture of what your bridge looks like on Handout 6.2.

11. **The Test:** We will test our designs in front of the whole class!

12. **After the Test:** Using Handout 6.2, draw a picture to share what your bridge looks like after the test.

13. What do you wonder now?

LONDON BRIDGE RECORDING SHEET

Directions: Circle the shapes you plan to use in your bridge design. Then draw a picture of your bridge before and after the test.

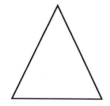

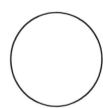

Before

After

WHAT'S HAPPENING IN THIS STEAM INVESTIGATION?

	Teacher	Student
Looks Like	- Moving around the room observing group work - Listening to student language, making notes of vocabulary or curiosity catchphrases used (nonevaluative)	- Planning, designing, sketching, and creating a bridge - Listening to and watching group members as they work together - Recording findings on Handout 6.2
Sounds Like	- Choral reading "London Bridge" - Modeling vocabulary and the curiosity catchphrase while observing group work - Asking questions to require students to dig deeper, make connections, or try again	- Choral reading "London Bridge" - Sharing learning using the curiosity catchphrase "*Oops, I learned . . .*" - Using vocabulary (*heavy, light, shape, triangle, bridge*) while creating the bridge - Sharing ideas, mistakes, and new learning with teacher and classmates

EXPLORATION

7

Old King Cole: *Sound and Vibration*

Old King Cole was a merry old soul,

And a merry old soul was he;

He called for his pipe, and he called for his bowl,

And he called for his fiddlers three.

Every fiddler he had a fiddle,

And a very fine fiddle had he;

Oh there's none so rare, as can compare,

With King Cole and his fiddlers three.

STEAM CHALLENGE

Old King Cole has a really big problem. His fiddlers three only have enough fiddles for two. And on top of that, his court has grown tired of listening to only violins day in and day out. It's a good thing innovators like you have shown up at the castle. Create an instrument for the third fiddler to play that will break up the same ole', same ole' at Old King Cole's court.

Goals and Objectives

During this exploration, students will:
- ask wondering questions to guide their investigation,
- investigate to discover the concept of vibration, and
- discuss with peers how string or rubber band instruments create sound.

Materials

- Handout 7.1: Student's Toolbox
- Rubber bands (all sizes)
- Plastic food storage containers
- Small plastic boxes
- Cardboard boxes
- Craft sticks
- Paint sticks
- Duct tape
- Scotch tape
- Scissors
- Handmade example instruments (rubber bands stretched across various-sized boxes)
- String instruments (e.g., guitar, banjo, mandolin, violin)

Note. You can display handmade rubber band instruments, toys, or actual instruments. Don't let this list intimidate you; it is fine if you only use the homemade box instruments.

Important Investigation Ideas to Note

In this challenge, students will be exploring sound and how it is created. By observing how the strings on these instruments move, they will notice that several things can impact the sounds we hear, like the length and width of the string (or rubber band) and the size of the box. They will also discover that vibration creates sound by playing with various instruments and by touching their throats and lips as they hum to feel the vibration. Students will use "*I wonder . . .*" to guide the investigation as they try out different materials to achieve the desired sound.

This lesson is set up as mini-Makerspace. Although you will have sample instruments that students can play with and explore to research ideas, there is not one right way to make these instruments. This mini-Makerspace process is similar to how students researched, planned, chose materials, wondered, explored, and tested in Exploration 6: London Bridge. You will release a little more control to the students during this exploration. If you feel that the materials list is too long for your students, it can be simplified to only boxes and rubber bands. Remember that the important thing in this experience is the thinking process, not the aesthetics of the instrument, and an instrument can be created with only two materials. Make this manageable to work in your classroom. Lastly, this mini-Makerspace works really well as a family event because it is something parents and children can easily replicate at home. If you have an upcoming family event at your school, consider making instruments!

Language and Literacy

Curiosity Catchphrase

- *I wonder . . .*

Vocabulary

- Sound
- Vibration

Speaking and Listening

- Who is this nursery rhyme about?
  - Choral read the poem or sing it together as a class.

- The rhyme says, "Old King Cole was a merry old soul." Ask if anyone knows what the word *merry* means in this sentence. If no one knows, tell students that merry means the same thing as happy. Draw a word web on the board and have the class brainstorm other words that would mean the same as merry as you add them to the board.
    - Partner Talk: The rhyme says, "Old King Cole was a merry old soul." What do you think this means?

- What is this nursery rhyme about?
    - Partner Talk: A *fiddle* is another word for a violin. What do you think is happening in this nursery rhyme? (They are having a party with music.)

EDUCATOR'S TOOLBOX

Introduction

- Choral read the poem again, but this time hand out the instruments first. (You do not need every student to have an instrument, and they can be real or homemade box instruments.) Tell the students you want them to strum along with you while you chant the rhyme. Ask the class to put on "engineer eyes and ears" to look and listen closely to the instruments while they play.
- Partner Talk: What did you notice happening to your instruments while you played? (The strings moved; there was sound.)
- Have the students strum the instruments again with their partners, but this time tell them you want them to describe with words what they notice with their "engineer eyes." So, this time instead of just saying the string moved, a student may say the string moved very fast. Guide the students to noticing the pattern that every time a string vibrates there is sound.
- Tell them this time you want them to use their "engineer ears" to listen. Have them close their mouths tightly and hum the tune of the rhyme with their fingers pressed against their lips or throat. Ask them

to describe what they felt while they were humming. Students who do not know the word *vibration* will often talk about movement.

- Introduce the word *vibration* to the students. Say: *We have noticed a pattern. What happens every time we hear sound?* (Vibration.) Tell the students that they are going to test that idea again. Have them strum their instruments (or watch as a friend strums) to see if there is movement, or vibration, every time there is sound.

- Say: *So what do we predict creates sound?* (Vibration.)

- Hold up a large box. Remind students of the catchphrase *"I wonder..."* and tell them that they will be using it to plan their investigation. Let the students watch you select a large and a small rubber band from the materials. Stretch the large rubber band around the box, and then stretch the small rubber band next to it.

- Ask the students if they predict the sounds will be the same or different. Strum each rubber band. Tell the students to use "engineer eyes and ears" one more time as they watch each of the strings move.

- Partner Talk: What did you notice about the sound the smaller rubber band made? (It makes a higher sound and vibrates faster.)

- Partner Talk: What did you notice about the sound the larger rubber band made? (It makes a lower sound and vibrates slower.)

- Say: *Think like an engineer: If I want to create an instrument that has only high-pitched sounds, what type of rubber bands should I use on this box? What if I want to create deeper sounds?*

- If you have access to a real string instrument like a guitar, let students make observations about the differences in the thickness of the strings and the sounds they make. They will notice the same pattern they found on the box string instrument.

- Tell the students that they were right earlier when they said that Old King Cole is having a party with his fiddlers, but he's run into trouble and needs their help.

- Read the STEAM challenge card to the students (see Appendix).

Investigation Procedure

1. Tell the students that today you have set up a music Makerspace in the classroom. Tell them makers are innovators. They solve problems, like the one the king has, by creating!

2. Have students tell you what they have learned about sound that can help them solve this problem for the king. (Vibration creates sound, and the size of the string impacts pitch.)

3. Partner Talk: How will you know that you have created a good instrument for the king? (Write these ideas down for the class. These will be each student's goals for his or her instrument.)

4. Distribute Handout 7.1: Student's Toolbox to guide students' investigations.

5. Show students the materials that will be available to them to create their instruments. Let students first select their box and then add additional materials, as the size of the box will determine the size of the rubber bands.

6. Tell students that while they are working to create their own instrument, they still may need to work together. For example: *Duct tape is very strong and is sometimes easier to work with if you have a friend to help you position and cut it on your instrument.*

7. Model an "*I wonder . . .*" statement for the class that would help them create their instruments. You could say: *I wonder if I could make an instrument that makes both deep and high-pitched sounds using a small box.* Based on that statement, have students tell you what materials you would need.

8. Tell the students that their "*I wonder . . .*" catchphrases will help them determine the materials they need to collect.

9. Partner Talk: Have students share "*I wonder . . .*" statements with a friend and verbally make a plan of what materials they will need.

10. Students may request different materials than what they previously asked for after they begin creating. That is great; it shows they are problem solving.

11. If students finish early, ask them what they wonder now that they have made an instrument using a box and a rubber band. A student might say, "I wonder if I could make an instrument that has an even deeper sound." Encourage him or her to go back to the materials and test that wondering. This is an investigation that could be ongoing—there really shouldn't be any "fast finishers." They just need to keep thinking of ways to innovate and make their design better and better!

Reflect

- Let the students share their instruments and their *"I wonder..."* catchphrases that they used to design their instruments.
- After they have created their instruments, have them look back at the list they made in step 3 of the Investigation Procedure (see p.94) and compare their instruments to the list. For example, if the list says that the instrument should have at least three different sounds, they will check to be sure their instruments make three different sounds.
- You might want to give students time to go back and modify their designs after this reflection.

Wonder

- Ask the students to tell you what they wonder now that they've designed, created, and tested this instrument. They might say something like, "I made a guitar from a box, but now I wonder if I could make a violin."
- Adding the materials for this lesson in your music or science center will give students the opportunity to test out their wonderings on another day.

Additional Literature Connections and Resources

Moss, L. (2000). *Zin! Zin! Zin! A violin.* New York, NY: Aladdin.
     This whimsical picture book offers young readers an introduction to musical instruments and groups. It also incorporates counting concepts connected to music.

Yamada, K. (2016). *What do you do with a problem?* Seattle, WA: Compendium.
     What Do You Do With a Problem? is a unique picture book that offers children an opportunity to learn how to face challenges, persevere, and problem solve to overcome obstacles.

STUDENT'S TOOLBOX

👁 **ENGINEER EYES:**
Notice how the rubber bands vibrate as they create sound.

👂 **ENGINEER EARS:**
Listen to the sounds the different rubber bands make. Listen for a friend's "*I wonder* . . ." phrases and engineer words like *sound* and *vibration*.

1. Welcome to Old King Cole's Music Makerspace!

2. **Share your ideas:** How will you know that you've created a good instrument for King Cole?

3. Take a look at the materials that you can use.

4. Think about your materials and how they can be used to make sound.

5. **Partner Talk:** Share your catchphrase, "*I wonder* . . ." (e.g., "I wonder if I can create a guitar using a large box and three rubber bands.").

6. **Partner Talk:** Make a plan for the materials you will need.

7. Gather your materials.

8. Design, create, and investigate!

9. Notice what type of sounds the smaller, thinner rubber bands make and what type of sounds the larger, thicker rubber bands make.

10. When you have finished with your design, take a look at our class list of the ways we will know that we've made a good instrument for King Cole. Compare your instrument to the list. If you want to make changes, feel free to do so.

11. What do you wonder now? How could you innovate to make your design even better?

Name: _____ Date: _____

WHAT'S HAPPENING IN THIS STEAM INVESTIGATION?

	Teacher	Student
Looks Like	- Moving around the room observing group work - Listening to student language, making notes of vocabulary or curiosity catchphrases used (nonevaluative)	- Planning, designing, creating, and testing the instrument - Listening to and watching classmates or partners as they work together and partner talk
Sounds Like	- Choral reading "Old King Cole" - Modeling vocabulary and curiosity catchphrase while observing group work - Asking questions to require students to dig deeper, make connections, or try again	- Choral reading "Old King Cole" - Sharing curiosity and planning using the catchphrase, "*I wonder . . .*" - Using vocabulary (*sound* and *vibration*) while creating instruments - Sharing ideas, mistakes, and new learning with teacher and classmates

EXPLORATION 7: OLD KING COLE

EXPLORATION

8

Five Little Speckled Frogs: *Buoyancy*

Five little speckled frogs

Sat on a speckled log

Eating the most delicious bugs (yum, yum)

One jumped into the pool

Where it was nice and cool

Then there were four speckled frogs (glub, glub).

Four little speckled frogs

Sat on a speckled log

. . . continues on the next page

. . . continued.

Eating the most delicious bugs (yum, yum)

One jumped into the pool

Where it was nice and cool

Then there were three speckled frogs (glub, glub).

Three little speckled frogs

Sat on a speckled log

Eating the most delicious bugs (yum, yum)

One jumped into the pool

Where it was nice and cool

Then there were two speckled frogs (glub, glub).

Two little speckled frogs

Sat on a speckled log

Eating the most delicious bugs (yum, yum)

One jumped into the pool

Where it was nice and cool

Then there was one speckled frog (glub, glub).

One little speckled frog

Sat on a speckled log

Eating the most delicious bugs (yum, yum)

One jumped into the pool

Where it was nice and cool

Then there were zero speckled frogs (glub, glub).

STEAM CHALLENGE

These little speckled frogs have a big problem. Their log isn't strong enough to hold all five frogs. One by one, the little speckled frog family is diving into the pool to save one another. Lucky for them, an engineer like you is nearby with the heart to help. Your challenge is to design a raft strong enough to hold all five speckled frogs.

Goals and Objectives

During this exploration, students will:
- make predictions to guide their exploration using the "*I think if . . .*" catchphrase,
- investigate to explore the concept of buoyancy in order to build schema, and
- design, create, and test a boat to see if it holds five frogs.

Materials

Note. Materials listed are needed per small group of students.
- Handout 8.1: Student's Toolbox
- Handout 8.2: Five Little Speckled Frogs Recording Sheet
- Five plastic frogs or stones
- Aluminum foil
- Straws
- Duct tape
- Glue
- Scissors
- Large clear plastic tub (demonstration)
- Various objects to test buoyancy (see p. 104)
- Water

Important Investigation Ideas to Note

This investigation offers students the opportunity to explore the idea of buoyancy by problem solving for the frogs and creating a flotation device.

Young students are often fascinated with the concept of buoyancy; this is why bath and pool toys have remained consistent childhood toys throughout the years. Buoyancy is the upward force on an object that allows it to sink (negative buoyancy), float (positive buoyancy), or stay suspended in the middle (neutral buoyancy). When you ask students why something sinks, they might tell you it is because of its mass; however, mass is only one part of the equation. The idea that a stone will sink but a very large ship will float helps them understand this idea. In order to determine buoyancy, you need to look at the relationship between mass and volume, or density (density = mass / volume).

This lesson is set up as mini-Makerspace, similar to Exploration 7: Old King Cole. As with the previous lesson, if you feel that the materials list is too long for your students, it can be simplified to one material: aluminum foil. Using only aluminum foil, students can create a boat! The number of materials isn't important; the planning, designing, creating, and thinking matter most. Make this manageable for your classroom.

Language and Literacy

Curiosity Catchphrase

- *I think if . . .*

Vocabulary

- Sink
- Float
- Buoyancy—negative, positive, and neutral

Speaking and Listening

- Nursery rhyme pattern
  - Sing or choral read the rhyme together as a class.
  - Tell the students you have noticed a pattern in this poem and in several of the other poems the class has investigated.
  - Work as a class to circle the pairs of rhyming words in this poem.
  - You might want to think back to other rhymes the students have read in their investigations, like "Hey Diddle Diddle," and discuss pairs of rhyming words in those poems.

- What is this nursery rhyme about?
  - The rhyme is about five little speckled frogs that eat bugs and hang out in the pond. For some reason they start jumping in the water.
  - Partner Talk: This rhyme, or song, has been around a very long time, and it is a great mystery. Until today no one knew why these frogs might be jumping in the water. Why might these frogs be jumping in the water? (Answers will vary.)

EDUCATOR'S TOOLBOX

Introduction

- Tell the students that the challenge today solves the mystery of why the frogs have been jumping in the water. Read the STEAM challenge card aloud to the students (see Appendix).
- Tell the students that you want to show them what happened to the frogs. Pull out a clear tub filled with water. Take a piece of aluminum foil, roll it like a log, and place it on the water. Create it so that it floats (positive buoyancy) or stays suspended in the water (neutral buoyancy), but when you add multiple frogs it will sink. Let the students count with you as you add the frogs.
- Partner Talk: What did you notice happening to the log as we added each frog? (It started to sink lower into the water.)
- Say: *So I wonder if you could use this same aluminum foil to create a raft for the frogs that would float. Do you think that might be possible?*
- Remind the students of when they looked at types of bridges before they designed London Bridge in Exploration 6. Ask them how that was helpful to them as they designed their own bridge. Tell them that they are going to research a science concept called *buoyancy* to help them develop a design for their frog raft. Students most likely have heard of the words *sink* and *float*; draw an illustration or diagram to show them how those words are connected to the idea of buoyancy (see Figure 1).

Buoyancy Mini-Lesson 1

- Have the students feel and describe the following objects, predict if they will float, test them, and tell you (or a partner) what they notice. If

FIGURE 1. Example buoyancy illustration.

you want to increase the vocabulary here, you can ask them to describe (or you can model for them) what happens, using the words *positive buoyancy*, *negative buoyancy*, and *neutral buoyancy*.

- Apple
- Wooden blocks
- Stones
- Bath toys (rubber ducks, boats, plastic frogs)
- Rubber ball
- Sponge
- Sponge filled with water

- Partner Talk: Think about the last test with the sponge. At first it floated, and then it sank. Why do you think that happened? (When the sponge was filled with water it was heavier.)

- Say: *We are thinking that the mass (or the amount of matter) of an object can help us know if it will sink or float, right?* Then add: *You are correct, but mass isn't the only thing that lets us know if the object will sink or float. Let's investigate that for a second.*

Buoyancy Mini-Lesson 2

- Pull out two sheets of aluminum foil. Tell the students the two sheets of foil are the same. Ask a student to hold the two sheets and describe to the class that they have the same mass. Have another student come up and crumple one of the sheets into a tight ball. Remind the students that the only change was physical; it is still the same sheet of foil and will weigh the same. You can pass it around to let students compare the sheet to the ball of foil. Ask the students to predict if the ball will float, test it, and tell you (or a partner) what they notice.
- Partner Talk: *We know that both the foil sheet and the foil ball were the same mass, but the ball sank, or had negative buoyancy. Why do you think this might have happened?* (The students might say something about size.)
- Add on to their ideas about size by connecting to the concept of volume and density. You can expand on this idea by adding that the foil sheet's mass was spread out across the water, while the foil ball was compacted into less space.
- Tell the students that although they are correct in thinking that mass does have a role in deciding if something will sink or float, so does volume, or the amount of space something takes up.
- The relationship between volume and mass is called *density*, and that concept is really important to engineers as they design boats to carry people, goods, or, in our case, frogs.
- Show the students a picture of a large barge floating on the water. Ask if they predict it is heavy. (In other words, could you lift it?) Ask them to describe what the barge is doing on the water. (It floats, or has positive buoyancy.)
- Show the students a small stone. (If you are not using plastic frogs, this might also be one of the stones you are using to represent the frogs.) Ask the students the same questions as before. Ask if it is heavy and if they can lift it. Put it back in the water and ask them to describe what is happening. (It sinks, or has negative buoyancy.)

- Put the stone and the illustration or diagram you created earlier (see p. 103) next to each other so students can compare and identify that the stone sank and has negative buoyancy.
- Partner Talk: We see that even though the boat has a greater mass, it floats, while the much smaller stone sinks. Talk about how this is similar to what happened to the aluminum foil.
- Say: *Now that you know about buoyancy, how will this help you create a boat for our frogs?* (We need to create a boat that floats, or has positive buoyancy.)

Investigation Procedure

1. Show students the materials that will be available to them to create their boats. Remind them that more materials do not always equal a better boat. Students may create their boats in pairs or small groups.

2. Tell the students that the catchphrase *"I'm thinking if . . ."* can help them make plans or test new ideas, just like *"I wonder . . ."* helped them create their instrument for Old King Cole.

3. Model an *"I'm thinking if . . ."* statement to the class to help build a boat: *I'm planning to create my boat from only two aluminum foil sheets, and I'm thinking if I fold up the sides of the boat so they are half as high as the frogs (or stones), it will help protect the boat from taking on water.* Then take your foil sheets and fold up the sides of the foil to make a boat.

4. Ask the class if anyone else has an *"I'm thinking if . . ."* idea to help them create their boats. Invite students to share any ideas they have. Respect their ideas and give them a try, even if you know they will not work.

5. Distribute Handout 8.1: Student's Toolbox to help guide their investigations.

6. Partner Talk: Have students share an *"I'm thinking if . . ."* statement with a friend and verbally make a plan of what materials they will need.

7. Before students begin creating, remind them about the previous catchphrase, *"Oops, I learned . . ."* Tell them that at some point in their investigation they will make a mistake, and that is great. It means they are challenging their brains! They can learn from it, clean up, and move forward.

8. Leave the five frogs (or stones) and the "pond" or tub out in the front of the room. Allow students to test their designs midway through their

boat creation if they choose. Encouraging students to do this midway through helps them learn from any mistakes they've made. They can then correct or enhance their design. (If you have a large class, it might be helpful to have several sets of frogs and a second tub of water.)

9. If students finish early, ask them to do another test and see how they might improve their design.

Reflect

- Let students complete one final test where they come up either in small groups or with the whole class to test their boat or raft with all five frogs. The students will reflect on their design each time they test it in the water and have the opportunity to say, *"I'm thinking if . . ."* and then correct or adapt their design.
- Using Handout 8.2: Five Little Speckled Frogs Recording Sheet, have the students sketch a picture sharing what happened to the boat during the test. Using the recording sheet, the students can cut out the frogs and glue them on to the sketch to show what happened to the frogs.
- Ask students if they believe they have solved this challenge (i.e., created a boat to hold all five frogs). Ask them how they know they did (or did not) succeed in this mission.
- This lesson offers students the opportunity to see that reflection does not just occur at the end of an investigation, but during the entire time they are planning, designing, and creating.

Wonder

- Ask the students to tell you what they wonder now that they've designed, created, and tested this boat for the frogs. For example: "I made a raft for the frogs from straws and duct tape that held all five frogs. Now, I'm wondering if I can create a boat that holds 10 frogs."
- Adding the materials for this lesson in your science center will give students the opportunity to test out their wonderings on another day.

Additional Literature Connections and Resources

De Séve, R. (2014). *Toy boat.* New York, NY: Philomel Books.
   This book for young children shares the story of a little boy and the boat he created from found materials.

Yamada, K. (2014). *What do you do with an idea?* Seattle, WA: Compendium.
   What Do You Do With an Idea? is an inspiring story that shares one child's experience with bringing an idea to life.

STUDENT'S TOOLBOX

👁	**ENGINEER EYES:** Watch what your boat does in water. Does it float, sink, or remain neutral? Look for problems and solutions!
👂	**ENGINEER EARS:** Listen for friends sharing ideas using engineer words, like *buoyancy*, *sink*, and *float*, and today's catchphrase, "*I'm thinking if . . .*"

1. Welcome to Speckled Frogs Pond! Take a look at the materials that you can use.

2. Think about your materials. How can they be used to create a boat or a raft that will safely hold all five frogs?

3. **Partner Talk:** Share the catchphrase "*I'm thinking if . . .*" to help you plan your design (e.g., "I'm thinking if I leave a large flat space on the bottom of my foil boat, it will give me plenty of room for the five frogs to sit.").

4. **Partner Talk:** Make a plan for materials that you will need.

5. Gather your materials.

6. Design, create, and investigate!

7. You may test your boat one time as you are creating to check for any problems.

8. Use the catchphrase "*I'm thinking if . . .*" as you problem solve.

9. Remember the catchphrase "*Oops, I learned . . .*" if your boat doesn't do what you want it to. This is just a chance to learn and try something different!

10. Get ready. When you have finished your boat, we will test it one last time together!

11. Fill out Handout 8.2 to share your investigation results.

12. What do you wonder now?

FIVE LITTLE SPECKLED FROGS RECORDING SHEET

Directions: Draw a picture to share what happened in your boat test. Then, cut out the number of frogs your boat held and glue them to your picture.

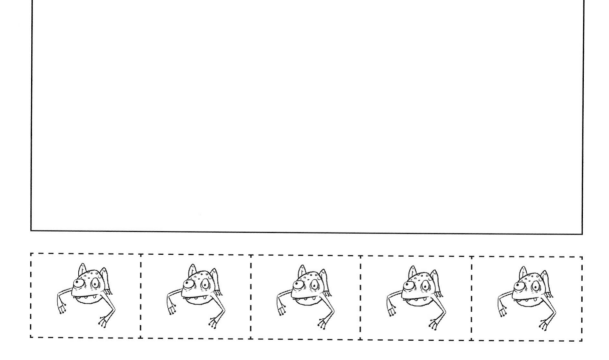

Name: _____ Date: _____

WHAT'S HAPPENING IN THIS STEAM INVESTIGATION?

	Teacher	Student
Looks Like	- Moving around the room observing group work - Listening to student language, making notes of vocabulary or curiosity catchphrases used (nonevaluative)	- Planning, designing, creating, and testing the boat - Listening to and watching classmates or partners as they work together and partner talk
Sounds Like	- Choral reading "Five Little Speckled Frogs" - Modeling vocabulary and the curiosity catchphrase while observing group work - Asking questions to require students to dig deeper, make connections, or try again	- Choral reading "Five Little Speckled Frogs" - Sharing curiosity and planning using the catchphrase "*I'm thinking if . . .*" - Using vocabulary (*buoyancy*, *sink*, and *float*) while creating the product - Sharing ideas, mistakes, and new learning with teacher and classmates

EXPLORATION 8: FIVE LITTLE SPECKLED FROGS

EXPLORATION

9

Star Light, Star Bright: *Density*

Star light, star bright

First star I see tonight

I wish I may

I wish I might

Have this wish

I wish tonight!

STEAM CHALLENGE

Of all the luck—a cloudy night! You know what that means: There's not a star in sight. How in the world will we have our wish? Tonight, we take luck into our own hands and make our own glowing light!

Goals and Objectives

During this exploration, students will:
- recognize mistakes and communicate new learning related to those mistakes,
- investigate the concept of density to build schema, and
- develop and record a plan for creating their own density bottles.

Materials

- Handout 9.1: Student's Toolbox
- Handout 9.2: Star Light, Star Bright Recording Sheet
- Density demonstration
  - 1-quart mason jar
  - 1/2 cup honey
  - 1/2 cup whole milk
  - 1/2 cup dish soap
  - 1/2 cup water
  - 1/2 cup vegetable oil
  - 1/2 cup white vinegar
  - Food coloring (optional)
  - 6 clear plastic cups

- Loose parts flashlight
  - 1 flashlight per group, dismantled into parts: battery, lid, and handle
  - 1 tray or container

- Star Wish Bottles
  - 1 clear plastic craft bottle per student (*Note.* If you prefer to recycle a bottle, small plastic spice bottles or thick, smooth plastic water bottles work best.)

- • Water
- • Baby oil
- • Vegetable oil
- • Glitter
- • Jars and containers
- • Small funnel
- • Food coloring

- – Tools
  - • Plastic gloves
  - • 6 turkey basters (or use one and rinse it in between each use)

Important Investigation Ideas to Note

In Exploration 8: Five Little Speckled Frogs, students noticed that the denser the object, the more likely it was to sink. In this investigation, students will continue exploring the same concept by observing a liquid density tower. Liquid towers, sometimes called rainbow towers, are commonly used with older students (see Additional Literature Connections and Resources). For our demonstration, we will use only ingredients that younger students have probably seen in their homes. In this investigation, students will notice that the denser the liquid, the closer it is to the bottom, while the less dense materials stay near the top.

Density describes how close together the molecules are in an object, or how much mass is in a given amount of space (density = mass / volume). Students became curious about the concept of density in the buoyancy challenge with Five Little Speckled Frogs. This lesson allows students to continue to investigate this concept while they create their own Star Wish Bottles and observe the different layers of liquid in their bottles. Students will also notice that the liquids flow differently as they are being poured into their bottles. This is the property of viscosity and is sometimes confused with density. Viscosity is the thickness of a fluid or resistance to pouring. For example, water has a low viscosity, while honey has a high viscosity.

Language and Literacy

Curiosity Catchphrase

- *Oops, I learned . . .*

Vocabulary

- Density
- Viscosity (thick, thin)
- Liquid

Speaking and Listening

- What is rhythm or meter?
  - Choral read the rhyme together as a class.
  - As you chant the poem together, invite students to clap out the rhythm with you.
  - Ask students to tell you what they notice about the way we read these nursery rhymes. (It has a flow or a beat.)
  - Tell the students that in poetry we call this beat *rhythm* or *meter*, and it is another special writing technique, like rhyme, that authors use.
  - Challenge the students to share another poem from the unit. Chant the rhyme and clap out the rhythm together.

- What is this nursery rhyme about?
  - Partner Talk: What is this poem about? (A person making a wish on a star.)
  - Partner Talk: People often say you can wish on a shooting star or the first star you see out at night. What do you think you might wish for? (Answers will vary.)

EDUCATOR'S TOOLBOX

Introduction

- Begin by having a few students share what they would have wished for if they were the author of this poem.

- Read the STEAM challenge card aloud to the class (see Appendix). Ask students: *How would you feel if you had your wish ready, but the stars were hidden by the clouds all night?* Continue: *Because we don't have stars to wish on tonight, would you like to take on this challenge and create your own Star Wish Bottles?*

Density Mini-Lesson 1

- Tell the students that you had an "*Oops, I learned . . .*" moment that might help them plan their investigation. Get out a clear plastic cup and use the turkey baster to pour in a little vegetable oil. Tell the students you were cooking last night and you accidently spilled a little of your water in the bowl. Use the baster to squeeze a little water on top of the oil.
- Ask students to put on their "scientist eyes" and tell you what they notice about the oil and water. You can give it a gentle stir and let students watch it separate. (You may add a few drops of food coloring to the water to make this easier to see.)
- Model today's curiosity catchphrase: *Oops, I learned something new about liquids! I was thinking back to our buoyancy sink/float investigation with the speckled frogs, and it reminded me of just what I'm seeing here. Some liquids sink to the bottom, and others come up to the top.*
- Ask students to think about our last investigation. Why did some items sink while others floated? Remind them of the word *density*. Say: *Objects that were denser sank, while objects that were less dense floated.*
- Partner Talk: How does knowing about density help us understand what is happening in this container of vegetable oil and water? (The water is denser, and the vegetable oil is less dense. *Note.* This is sometimes a confusing concept for young children because vegetable oil is a thicker liquid than water, but it sits on top. We need to give young learners time to play and explore with various liquids as they are developing a schema. Investigations like this one will help children understand scientific concepts like density and viscosity in later years, because this exploration will provide an anchor experience.)

Density Mini-Lesson 2

- Tell the students that your "oops" moment made you wonder about other liquids you have at home. You decided to bring some in so you could learn together.

- Before class, have 1/2 of a cup of each of the liquid ingredients poured into small clear plastic cups. Be sure to label each cup. Point out the labels to the class. Hold up the clear vinegar and the clear water. Say: *These are two different ingredients, but they look a lot alike.* Ask the students to tell you why they think it is important for scientists to label their ingredients.
- Using the turkey baster, slowly add one ingredient at a time to the glass mason jar.
- Partner Talk: What did you notice happening as I added each liquid? (There are many different observations the students could make: The liquids stay in layers; the liquids are all different colors; some pour in quickly, and some move slowly.)

Density Mini-Lesson 3

- Say: *You may be wondering what all of these liquids have to do with our Star Wish Bottle, but I happened to be cooking next to a lamp, and I had on my "scientist eyes" and noticed something pretty interesting. I don't want to tell you, because I want you to see it for yourself! Because we don't have a lamp for everyone to use, I've brought in my flashlights.*
- Show the students one of your flashlight trays. Tell them that you like to keep your flashlights stored as loose parts because they work like a puzzle when you go to put them together. Tell the students they will have an opportunity to work with the loose parts to make the flashlight work.
- Put a flashlight together. You may want to put it together incorrectly the first time to model perseverance and learning from a mistake. Remind students that they may not get the parts right the first time they try, but that's just an "oops" they can learn from.
- Pour a little water in a cup and add food coloring. Get out a clear plastic bottle. Tell the students that scientists need to record, write down, or draw their plan. Show the students a page you are using to take notes.
- Have a student use the baster to squeeze in vegetable oil until the bottle is half full and then use another baster to slowly squeeze in water until the container is almost filled. Put the cap on the bottle very tightly.
- Turn off the lights and turn on the flashlight. Shine the flashlight under the Star Wish Bottle and turn it upside down. Let the students tell you what they notice happening. Turn the lights back on.

- Say: *If we turn the lights off and put our lights on the bottle, it seems to shine bright like a star. This made me wonder if I could make this bottle look even more star-like.* Take off the cap and invite the students to come up and add some glitter to the bottle.
- Put on gloves. Tell the students you are going to work with a material that could be harmful to your skin, so you will wear gloves. Also tell them that you will do this part for everyone. Superglue the lid onto the bottle and screw the lid on tightly.
- Turn the lights off, shine the flashlight under the bottle, and have the students chant the rhyme with you again.
- Partner Talk: Ask students to tell you what they notice is happening in the bottle. Challenge them to use the word *density* or *dense* in the description.
- Tell the students that your bottle is almost ready for wishing, but you want everyone to wish together!

Investigation Procedure

1. The students will come up to work in small groups. When students are not working with you, they will be working in the Flashlight Loose Part Lab to assemble the flashlights for the class. Remind students that today's catchphrase is *"Oops, I learned . . ."* but they are welcome to use any of the others they've learned in other lessons as well.

2. Distribute Handout 9.1: Student's Toolbox and Handout 9.2: Star Light, Star Bright Recording Sheet to the students. Start the investigation by letting everyone make a plan. Call a few students at a time to bring their plan back to you and create their Star Wish Bottles.

3. Organization: Have labeled jars of colored water, baby oil, and vegetable oil. Also have small containers and scoops of glitter. (A funnel might be helpful if the bottle has a small opening.)

4. Before they add each ingredient, let students share how much of each ingredient they plan to add, based on their plan (e.g., "I want my bottle to be about 1/2 red water and 1/2 baby oil"). Let the students add water, oil, and glitter to their bottles.

5. Students may notice some liquids pour in slowly, and others pour faster. This is evidence that liquids have different viscosities. Encourage the students to tell you what they notice about the liquids by sharing the speed at which they pour (fast or slow) and if they are thick or thin.

6. You might also have students describe what they see happening using relative location vocabulary like they did in Exploration 2: Did You Ever See a Lassie? (e.g., "The blue water is *above* the baby oil").

7. Have students work together as they create their bottle. For example, one student may hold the bottle while another uses the turkey baster to squeeze in water. If you are working with older students, you may let everyone in the small group work together in pairs to create their bottle.

8. If you are working with very young students, you might want to let students create their bottles one at a time. (Remember, you don't have to do this all in one class period or day.) The other students in the small group will notice and share observations, predictions, or wonderings.

9. As each student finishes his or her bottle, superglue the lid on. When each small group is finished, have them go back to work in the Flashlight Loose Part Lab to assemble the flashlights.

10. Continue with the process until all students have had a chance to plan, design, and create their bottles.

Reflect

- After all students have created their bottles, give each group one of the flashlights assembled in the Flashlight Loose Part Lab. Ask the students to tell you what they learned about putting together a flashlight while working in the Flashlight Loose Part Lab. (Answers will vary here. Students may discuss how the flashlight works or even mistakes they made while they were learning to put it together.)

- Give the students their bottles and turn off the lights. Chant or sing the rhyme again together as the students shake and shine the flashlights on their bottles.

- Tell students to make their wish.

- Turn the lights on, and have the students sketch a picture on Handout 9.2 sharing what their Star Wish Bottle looked like during the test and what they wished for.

Wonder

- Show the students your bottle again. Model thinking out loud for the students: *I notice that the oil and water separate back into layers if I leave it still. I'm wondering what would happen if I used more oil than water next time.*
- Partner Talk: Share with each other what you noticed and what you wonder now about your bottle.

Additional Literature Connections and Resources

Rosenthal, A. K. (2015). *I wish you more.* San Francisco, CA: Chronicle Books.
    Young children will explore the idea of wishing for things, like more ups than downs or more give than take, in this picture book.

Spangler, S. (2010). *Sick science: Amazing 9 layer density tower—SICK science! #012.* Retrieved from https://www.stevespanglerscience.com/lab/videos/amazing-9-layer-density-tower-sick-science-012
    Steve Spangler's "Amazing 9 Layer Density Tower" investigation expands on the concepts explored in this density investigation. This resource also gives a little more information on the scientific concepts investigated in a density tower.

Spangler, S. (2014). *Sugar rainbow.* Retrieved from https://www.stevespanglerscience.com/lab/experiments/sugar-rainbow
    The Sugar Rainbow investigation offers children an opportunity to create liquids of varying densities using only water, sugar, and food coloring.

STUDENT'S TOOLBOX

👁	**SCIENTIST EYES:** What do you notice happening to the liquids?
👂	**SCIENTIST EARS:** Listen for friends to share ideas using the catchphrase *"Oops, I learned . . ."* and scientist words like *thick, thin, liquid,* and *density.*

1. Are you excited to make your wish? We will wish together after everyone has created his or her bottle.

2. Make a plan on Handout 9.2.

3. This investigation will be done in two groups: "Flashlight Loose Part Lab" and "Creating Star Wish Bottles."

4. Flashlight Loose Part Lab
   a. Investigate and explore as you work to assemble the flashlights.
   b. Don't worry if you make a mistake and your flashlight doesn't light. Say, *"Oops, I learned . . ."* and give it another try.
   c. **Partner Talk:** What did you learn while putting together the flashlights?

5. Creating Star Wish Bottles
   a. Your teacher will call you to the table.
   b. Share your plan for creating your bottle.
   c. Create and explore as you add the ingredients to your bottle.
   d. **Partner Talk:** What do you notice as you create your bottle?

EXPLORATION 9: STAR LIGHT, STAR BRIGHT

6. Get ready. We are going to turn off the lights and make our wishes soon!

7. Draw a picture of what happened when you tested your Star Wish Bottle, using Handout 9.2.

8. What do you wonder now?

STAR LIGHT, STAR BRIGHT RECORDING SHEET

Directions: Circle the liquids you plan to use in your bottle. Write a fraction next to each bottle to represent how much of your bottle you want to be filled with each liquid.

EXPLORATION 9: STAR LIGHT, STAR BRIGHT

Name: _____ Date: _____

Sketch a picture of your Star Wish Bottle.

Name: _____ Date: _____

WHAT'S HAPPENING IN THIS STEAM INVESTIGATION?

	Teacher	Student
Looks Like	- Moving around the room observing group work - Listening to student language, making notes of vocabulary or curiosity catchphrases used (nonevaluative)	- Planning, designing, creating, and testing the Star Wish Bottle and problem solving in the Flashlight Loose Part Lab - Listening to and watching classmates or partners as they work together and partner talk
Sounds Like	- Choral reading "Star Light, Star Bright" - Modeling vocabulary and the curiosity catchphrase while observing group work - Asking questions to require students to dig deeper, make connections, or try again	- Choral reading "Star Light, Star Bright" - Sharing curiosity and planning using the catchphrase "*Oops, I learned . . .*" - Using vocabulary (*thick, thin, density,* and *liquid*) to describe processes during product creation - Sharing ideas, mistakes, and new learning with teacher and classmates

EXPLORATION 10

Baa, Baa, Black Sheep: *Color and Chromatography*

Baa, baa, black sheep,
Have you any wool?
Yes, sir, yes, sir,
Three bags full.
One for the master,
And one for the dame,
And one for the little boy
Who lives down the lane.

STEAM CHALLENGE

As if sharing three bags of wool isn't enough, now the seamstress called and wants more. She needs wool in colors other than black or white. The little black sheep says she can help because she was drawn in a marker, not pencil like the rest of her friends at Storybook Farm. She insists to the farmer that she hides more colors in her wool. The farmer is skeptical. Why should he believe this sheep? Are you ready to test and see if this little sheep is telling the truth?

Goals and Objectives

By the end of this exploration, students will be able to:
- connect to schema, or prior knowledge, to solve problems;
- investigate chromatography in order to build schema; and
- describe observations using vocabulary like *more*, *less*, *longest*, and *shortest*.

Materials

Note. Materials listed are needed per small group of students.
- Handout 10.1: Student's Toolbox
- Handout 10.2: Baa, Baa, Black Sheep Recording Sheet
- Coffee filters (one per student)
- Wax paper (one sheet per student)
- Spray bottles
- Pipettes or eyedroppers
- Wet wipes
- Black markers (water-soluble, not permanent; one per student)
- Water
- Cups, jars, or small buckets
- Plastic dishpans
- Plastic tablecloth
- Sheared wool (optional; can be obtained from local farmers or online craft markets)
- Wool garment

Important Investigation Ideas to Note

In Exploration 9: Star Light, Star Bright, students had the opportunity to see a density tower, where different liquids were layered on one another to create a rainbow effect. In this exploration, students will use one liquid—black ink—separated into many different colors. This process of separation, chromatography, literally means "color writing." This technique, developed in the early 1900s by Mikhail Tsvet to separate plant pigments for dyes, is commonly used today to test for unknown substances. Law enforcement officers use it to investigate crime scenes, and environmental engineers use this method to test for water and air pollution.

Although this investigation could be done using permanent markers and rubbing alcohol, because we are working with younger students, it is a good idea to use water-soluble markers. The ink in these markers washes off with water.

Language and Literacy

Curiosity Catchphrase

- *This reminds me of . . .*

Vocabulary

- Color words: black, red, blue, yellow, green, orange, purple, pink
- Chromatography
- More
- Less
- Longest
- Shortest

Speaking and Listening

- What is this nursery rhyme about?
  - Choral read the poem together.
  - Partner Talk: Who is this poem about? (A farmer and a black sheep.)
  - Partner Talk: Why might the farmer be asking the sheep if she has wool? How do we use wool today? (Answers will vary.)

- Having a sample of sheep's wool and a wool sweater or scarf for students to see might help students discuss why the farmer asked for wool.

- What is alliteration?
  - Ask the students to repeat the title, "Baa, Baa, Black Sheep" and then "Baa, Baa, Black." Have them tell you what they notice about those three words in the title. (All three words start with the letter B, or all of the words start with the same sound.)
  - Tell the students that when words sitting next to each other, or close to one another, start with the same letter or the same sound, this is called *alliteration*, and it is often used in poetry, character names, and titles.
  - Alliteration is one of those long words that are a mouthful for young students. Let them practice the word. Remember: The goal is not for the students to have mastered the name of the vocabulary word here, but to build knowledge to help them make connections during later learning opportunities.
  - Brainstorm examples of alliteration that the students are familiar with:
    - ▶ Mickey Mouse
    - ▶ Peter Parker (Spiderman)
    - ▶ *The Butter Battle Book* by Dr. Seuss

EDUCATOR'S TOOLBOX

Introduction

- Read the STEAM challenge card aloud to the class (see Appendix). Ask students to think back to the Star Light, Star Bright investigation and the colorful density tower they created with different liquids. Tell the students that in that lesson you used different colored liquids to make a colorful tower.
- Hold up a black marker and ask them if they think it is possible to take one color and make many colors. Poll the class, asking students if they

believe it is possible for the black sheep to be drawn with a marker that hides many colors.

- Model today's curiosity catchphrase: *This reminds me of a time when I was painting. I got some yellow paint without rinsing off my blue, and guess what color it made?* (Green.) If students have had limited experiences with color mixing, you can show them this process quickly, using markers on a sheet of paper as you "remember."
- Partner Talk: Remember and share a time when you have seen colors mix to make another color (e.g., Play-Doh mixing, mustard and ketchup, finger paints, chocolate/strawberry milk, etc.).

Chromatography Mini-Lesson

- Say: *We know it is possible to combine colors to make other colors, but is it possible to separate those colors? Let's explore that idea today. Because the black sheep is black, I'm thinking that is the color we will use for our investigation.*
- Tell students you have heard of a process called *chromatography*, which means "color writing," that forensic scientists and police officers use to help solve crimes.
- Say: *I have the materials here that you need in order to use this process to investigate a black marker's ink.* Show the students the black markers, coffee filters, jars of water, and a variety of water tools (e.g., spray bottles, eyedroppers).
- Partner Talk: Let's make a plan together as a class. How do you think we could use these materials to test if the little black sheep really does hide other colors in her wool?
- Write a simple plan together on board. You can guide students to each step by looking at the materials together and asking questions: *I see we have black markers. I'm wondering what we have up here that we can draw on* (coffee filter). *Now that we have our circle on the paper, I'm wondering if there is anything that might help us separate these colors* (water). A sample plan might look like the following:
  - Share "*I wonder...*" statement with a friend.
  - Share prediction.
  - Gather materials.
  - Using the marker, draw a circle (or pattern) on the center of the coffee filter paper.
  - Put the coffee filter in a dishpan.

- Add water, using method of your choice.
- Transfer to wax paper to dry.
- Notice what happens.
- Learn, share, and wonder!

Investigation Procedure

1. Distribute Handout 10.1: Student's Toolbox and Handout 10.2: Baa, Baa, Black Sheep Recording Sheet. Ask students to record their prediction by checking the box and circle the type of water tool they will need.

2. Pass out the materials. (*Note.* Plastic shower caddies are a good way to organize these materials.)
   a. Pass out a dishpan for each student (or group of students, if you want them to take turns).
   b. Give each student a sheet of wax paper. Tell them that when their filter is wet, they will put it on the wax paper to dry.
   c. Pass out dishpans with cups of water for the eyedroppers and spray bottles of water.

3. Remind students to look at their plan and share a wondering question that will guide their experiment.

4. Have the students draw a circle (or pattern) on the paper and then put it in the dishpan. (They may need to take turns using the dishpan.)

5. Play, explore, and learn!

6. As the students are adding water, you might walk around modeling "*This reminds me of . . .*" statements or asking students to tell you what this investigation reminds them of. They might remember a time when a paper got wet and the ink smeared across the page or a time that they accidently mixed colors. Any connections students share help them better understand what they see happening. You might also ask students to share their wondering question or their observation.

7. Students might feel frustrated. Remember to give them wait time and let them think. Rather than solving the problem for them, give them an opportunity to think through it first. For example, a student may feel frustrated that the water doesn't come out of the spray bottle correctly. Rather than fixing the sprayer, you can say: *That is a problem. I wonder what part of the bottle is controlling how the water comes out.* By

thinking through this and solving the problem on his or her own, or at least thinking through it with you, the student will begin to see him- or herself as someone who can solve problems rather than someone who depends on others.

8. Continue with the process until all students have had a chance to add water to their filters. After students have sprayed the paper, have them transfer it to wax paper while they watch what happens.

9. Have the students help you tidy up the area, cleaning up any water that may have spilled. Wet wipes are a great cleanup tool for this investigation.

Reflect

- When the students have put their creations away to dry and helped to clean up their area, have them draw a picture of what they see on their coffee filter now on Handout 10.2.

- Partner Talk: What happened when we added water to our black drawing? (The colors moved up the paper.)

- Remind the students that this process is called chromatography. They used the water to separate the colors (or dyes) used to create the color black.

- Also have them complete the reflection sentence on the Handout 10.2: "The black sheep hid _____ colors in her wool."

- Partner Talk: I wonder if the water application tool changes the results. Find a partner who used a different tool than you did.

- Discuss as a class or have students partner talk about the following questions:
  • Think back to our challenge. Was the black sheep telling the truth?
  • Which color traveled the longest distance?
  • Which color traveled the shortest distance?
  • Which color do you see the most?
  • Which color do you see the least?
  • Which color was the most surprising?

Wonder

- Partner Talk: Share with each other what you noticed and what you wonder now about separating colors with water. (Answers will vary. Let several students share.)
- Model: *Wow. We've learned that black is made up of more than one color. Now I wonder if other colors might be made up of more than one color, and if we can separate the colors the same way we did with black.*
- Adding different colored markers, water, and coffee filters to your science or art center will give students the opportunity to continue investigating this idea.

Additional Literature Connections and Resources

Feldman, J. (2002). Baa baa black sheep. [Recorded by Dr. Jean Feldman]. On *Nursery rhymes and good ol' times* [CD]. Charleston, SC: Music Design.
    Dr. Jean's lively version of "Baa, Baa, Black Sheep" provides an engaging opportunity for children to sing and chant the nursery rhyme.

Tullet, H. (2014). *Mix it up.* San Francisco, CA: Chronicle Books.
    In this interactive picture book, young children will have the opportunity to explore color mixing as they follow the author's instruction to mix up the colors on the page.

STUDENT'S TOOLBOX

👁	**SCIENTIST EYES:** What do you notice happening to the black marker ink?
👂	**SCIENTIST EARS:** Listen for friends to share ideas using the catchphrase *"This reminds me of . . ."* and scientist words like *more, less, longest, shortest, chromatography,* and color words.

1. What do you think: Is the black sheep telling the truth? Record your prediction on Handout 10.2. Circle the water tool you plan to use in your experiment.

2. Gather your materials.

3. Draw a picture, shape, or pattern on your coffee filter using your black marker.

4. **Partner Talk:** Share your prediction with your friend.

5. Put the coffee filter in the dishpan. Then apply a little water using the water tool you selected on your plan.

6. **Partner Talk:** What do you notice happening?

7. Repeat steps 3–6 until everyone at your table has had a turn to add water to their filter.

8. Tidy up your area.

9. Draw a picture sharing what happened in your investigation and finish the sentence: "The black sheep hid _____ colors in her wool."

10. **Partner Talk:** I wonder if the water application tool changes the results. Find a partner who used a different tool than you did and compare your results.

11. What do you wonder now?

BAA, BAA, BLACK SHEEP RECORDING SHEET

Directions: Check the statement below that you believe to be true.

❑   I predict the black sheep hides colors in her wool.

❑   I predict the black sheep *does not* hide colors in her wool.

Circle the tool you plan to use in your investigation:

Draw a picture to share what happened in your investigation.

The black sheep hid _____ colors in her wool.

Name: _____ Date: _____

WHAT'S HAPPENING IN THIS STEAM INVESTIGATION?

	Teacher	Student
Looks Like	- Moving around the room observing group work - Listening to student language, making notes of vocabulary or curiosity catchphrases used (nonevaluative)	- Planning, creating, and testing chromatography - Listening to and watching classmates or partners as they work together and partner talk
Sounds Like	- Choral reading "Baa, Baa, Black Sheep" - Modeling vocabulary and the curiosity catchphrase while observing group work - Asking questions to require students to dig deeper, make connections, or try again	- Choral reading "Baa, Baa, Black Sheep" - Sharing curiosity and planning using the catchphrase, *"This reminds me of . . ."* - Using vocabulary (color words, *longest, shortest, more, less, chromatography*) to describe processes during product creation - Sharing ideas, mistakes, and new learning with teacher and classmates

REFERENCES

Bloom, B. (Ed.). (1956). *Taxonomy of educational objectives: The classification of educational goals. Handbook I: Cognitive domain*. New York, NY: Longman.

The Cockrell School of Engineering at the University of Texas at Austin. (n.d.). *Spatial visualization*. Retrieved from http://www.engr.utexas.edu/future/undergraduates/visualization

Fischer, K. (2011). *Interactive play develops kids' spatial skills*. Retrieved from https://news.temple.edu/news/interactive-play-develops-kids-spatial-skills

Francek, M. (2006). Promoting discussion in the science classroom using gallery walks. *NSTA WebNews Digest*. Retrieved from http://www.nsta.org/publications/news/story.aspx?id=52391

Harvey, S., & Goudvis, A. (2007). *Strategies that work: Teaching comprehension for understanding and engagement* (2nd ed.). Portland, ME: Stenhouse.

Maslow, A. H. (1943). A theory of human motivation. *Psychological Review, 50*, 370–396.

Peterson, R. (1992). *Life in a crowded place: Making a learning community*. Portsmouth, NH: Heinemann.

Project GEMS. (2011). Innovation model. *The Center for Gifted Studies at Western Kentucky University*. Retrieved from https://www.wku.edu/gifted/project_gems/innovation_model.php

Ricci, M. C. (2017). *Mindsets in the classroom: Building a growth mindset learning community* (Rev. ed.). Waco, TX: Prufrock Press.

Roberts, J. L., & Inman, T. F. (2015). *Strategies for differentiating instruction: Best practices for the classroom* (3rd ed.). Waco, TX: Prufrock Press.

Sheffield, L. J. (2003). *Extending the challenge in mathematics: Developing mathematical promise in K–8 students*. Thousand Oaks, CA: Corwin Press.

Simon, C. A. (n.d.). Using partner talk to strengthen student collaboration and understanding. *National Council of Teachers of English*. Retrieved from http://www.readwritethink.org/professional-development/strategy-guides/using-partner-talk-strengthen-30954.html

Stanford d.school. (n.d.) *A virtual crash course in design thinking*. Retrieved from https://dschool.stanford.edu/resources-collections/a-virtual-crash-course-in-design-thinking

Wagner, T. (2012). *Creating innovators: The making of young people who will change the world*. New York, NY: Simon & Schuster.

APPENDIX

Nursery Rhyme STEAM Challenge Cards

The STEAM challenge cards are provided as a tool to help engage children in the nursery rhyme and the problem they are helping the characters solve in each investigation. The cards can be used in many different ways. Put them in a box and encourage children to make predictions before reading the challenge aloud; copy them and send home to help children share their explorations with families; or enlarge them and post them as anchor charts in the classroom along with students' reflections or plans from the investigations. Basically, these cards were created to help you introduce the challenges, but they can be used in any way that is most helpful to you and the children you serve.

EXPLORATION 1: Hickory, Dickory, Dock

The chime is ringing. The clock struck one. The mice are panicked. Everyone knows the cat wakes to prowl the house at one o'clock. Yet, the mice can't seem to make it down the clock quick enough each night. They have started to use toy cars to zoom down the ramp, but they still can't seem to beat the cat. Your mission is to see if you can help the mice get down the clock ramp quickly and safely.

Hickory, dickory, dock,
The mouse ran up the clock,
The clock struck one,
The mouse ran down,
Hickory, dickory, dock.

EXPLORATION 2: Did You Ever See a Lassie?

Help! Lassie is in a new town, and the map app on her phone has gone haywire. Now she is lost! She's stuck going this way and that way. Your mission is to create a 3-D path to help Lassie find her way back home.

Did you ever see a lassie?
A lassie, a lassie?
Did you ever see a lassie
Go this way and that?
Go this way and that way,
Go this way and that way.
Did you ever see a lassie
Go this way and that?

EXPLORATION 3: Hey Diddle Diddle

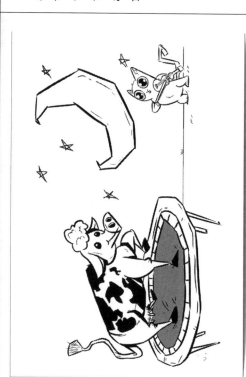

Hey diddle diddle,
The cat and the fiddle,
The cow jumped over the moon.
The little dog laughed,
To see such sport,
And the dish ran away with the spoon.

My goodness, that poor cow. He's out there jumping and jumping . . . and jumping. He just can't make it. But who can blame him? Have you ever tried to jump over the moon? Now the dog is laughing at him! Good thing the cow is friends with an engineer like you. Let's create a mini-trampoline and help that poor cow leap over the moon.

EXPLORATION 4: Rock-a-Bye, Baby

This sweet baby loves to rock in her treetop, but she needs your help. The last time she fell asleep she was holding her bottle upside down and noticed it made the most interesting patterns on the ground while she was sleeping. She'd hoped to get a closer look, but unfortunately, the cradle broke, she fell on the accidental artwork, and now it's gone forever. Her parents have put her back in the cradle, she's holding her bottle over the side again just like last time, but she's having a string of bad luck. First the cradle breaks, and now there's no wind! The baby will not stop crying because she really wants to see her rocking milk artwork again. Her parents are in desperate need of an engineer and an artist to make some more beautiful cradle artwork for their daughter. Will you be a dear engineer and make some cradle artwork that doesn't depend on wind?

Rock-a-bye, baby
In the treetop
When the wind blows
The cradle will rock
When the bough breaks
The cradle will fall
And down will come baby
Cradle and all.

Name: _____ Date: _____

EXPLORATION 5: Miss Mary Mack

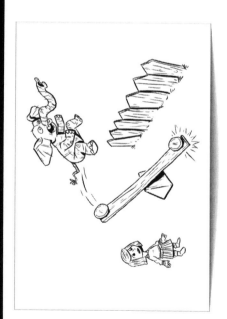

Miss Mary Mack, Mack, Mack

All dressed in black, black, black

With silver buttons, buttons, buttons

All down her back, back, back

She asked her mother, mother, mother

For fifty cents, cents, cents

To watch the elephant, elephant, elephant

Jump over the fence, fence, fence

He jumped so high, high, high

That he reached the sky, sky, sky

And he didn't come back, back, back

Until the Fourth of July, 'ly, 'ly!

The circus is in an uproar. The number one attraction, the fence-jumping elephant, Mr. Eli, had one too many peanuts at the last stop and can't make the jump! No one wants the beloved elephant to get hurt, and the ringmaster is threatening to cancel the show, but Mr. Eli is determined nothing will stop him from jumping the fence. His dear friend, Mary Mack, is all dressed up and has borrowed money from her mother to see the show. He does not want to let her down. Mr. Eli has heard that you are an engineer and wondered if you could design a contraption to help him leap over the fence. So, what do you say? Are you willing to help Mr. Eli?

EXPLORATION 6: London Bridge

London Bridge is falling down,
Falling down, falling down.
London Bridge is falling down,
My fair lady.

The bridge is falling down . . . falling down! Who wants to be on a bridge that is falling down? No one! *The Daily Times* reported that the bridge fell while a truck full of apples from the local orchard was crossing it. Don't worry. No one was hurt, but the city is desperate to make a plan for a new bridge that will not fall with a truck full of apples . . . or a car full of people! Thankfully, the city has architects and engineers like you to solve this problem. Design and create a new model of a bridge strong enough to hold nine apples to help your friends in London learn how to make a stronger bridge.

EXPLORATION 7: Old King Cole

Old King Cole has a really big problem. His fiddlers three only have enough fiddles for two. And on top of that, his court has grown tired of listening to only violins day in and day out. It's a good thing innovators like you have shown up at the castle. Create an instrument for the third fiddler to play that will break up the same ole', same ole' at Old King Cole's court.

Old King Cole was a merry old soul,
And a merry old soul was he;
He called for his pipe, and he called for his bowl,
And he called for his fiddlers three.

Every fiddler he had a fiddle,
And a very fine fiddle had he;
Oh there's none so rare, as can compare,
With King Cole and his fiddlers three

EXPLORATION 8: Five Little Speckled Frogs

These little speckled frogs have a big problem. Their log isn't strong enough to hold all five frogs. One by one, the little speckled frog family is diving into the pool to save one another. Lucky for them, an engineer like you is nearby with the heart to help. Your challenge is to design a raft strong enough to hold all five speckled frogs.

Five little speckled frogs
Sat on a speckled log
Eating the most delicious
   bugs (yum, yum)
One jumped into the pool
Where it was nice and cool
Then there were four
speckled frogs (glub, glub).
Four little speckled frogs
Sat on a speckled log

Eating the most delicious
   bugs (yum, yum)
One jumped into the pool
Where it was nice and cool
Then there were three
speckled frogs (glub, glub).
Three little speckled frogs
Sat on a speckled log
Eating the most delicious
   bugs (yum, yum)

Eating the most delicious
   bugs (yum, yum)
One jumped into the pool
Where it was nice and cool
Then there were two
speckled frogs (glub, glub).
Two little speckled frogs
Sat on a speckled log
Eating the most delicious
   bugs (yum, yum)
One jumped into the pool
Where it was nice and cool

Then there was one
speckled frog (glub, glub).
One little speckled frog
Sat on a speckled log
Eating the most delicious
   bugs (yum, yum)
One jumped into the pool
Where it was nice and cool
Then there were zero
speckled frogs (glub, glub).

EXPLORATION 9: Star Light, Star Bright

Of all the luck—a cloudy night! You know what that means: There's not a star in sight. How in the world will we have our wish? Tonight, we take luck into our own hands and make our own glowing light!

Star light, star bright
First star I see tonight
I wish I may
I wish I might
Have this wish
I wish tonight!

EXPLORATION 10: Baa, Baa, Black Sheep

As if sharing three bags of wool isn't enough, now the seamstress called and wants more. She needs wool in colors other than black or white. The little black sheep says she can help because she was drawn in a marker, not pencil like the rest of her friends at Storybook Farm. She insists to the farmer that she hides more colors in her wool. The farmer is skeptical. Why should he believe this sheep? Are you ready to test and see if this little sheep is telling the truth?

Baa, baa, black sheep,
Have you any wool?
Yes, sir, yes, sir,
Three bags full.
One for the master,
And one for the dame,
And one for the little boy
Who lives down the lane.

ABOUT THE AUTHOR

Allison Bemiss has worked to encourage innovative thinking in early childhood and elementary-age children for nearly 15 years, while serving as a teacher, interventionist, and education consultant. She currently works for The Center for Gifted Studies at Western Kentucky University as project coordinator for Little Learners, Big Ideas and for the Green River Regional Educational Cooperative developing workshops for early childhood and elementary educators. She can be contacted at https://www.littlelearnersbigideas.org.